THE MAKER PLAYBOOK

A Guide to Creating Inclusive Learning Experiences

CAROLINE D. HAEBIG

INTERNATIONAL SOCIETY FOR TECHNOLOGY IN EDUCATION
PORTLAND, OREGON • ARLINGTON, VIRGINIA

THE MAKER PLAYBOOK
A GUIDE TO CREATING INCLUSIVE LEARNING EXPERIENCES

Caroline D. Haebig

© 2021 International Society for Technology in Education

World rights reserved. No part of this book may be reproduced or transmitted in any form or by any means—electronic, mechanical, photocopying, recording, or by any information storage or retrieval system—without prior written permission from the publisher. Email permissions@iste.org for more information.

Senior Director of Books and Journals: *Colin Murcray*
Senior Acquisitions Editor: *Valerie Witte*
Development and Copy Editor: *Linda Laflamme*
Proofreader: *Lisa Hein*
Indexer: *Valerie Haynes Perry*
Book Design and Production: *Danielle Foster*
Cover Design: *Christina DeYoung*

Library of Congress Cataloging-in-Publication Data
Names: Haebig, Caroline, author.
Title: The maker playbook : a guide to creating inclusive learning experiences / Caroline Haebig.
Description: First edition. | Portland, Oregon : International Society for Technology in Education, [2021] | Includes bibliographical references and index.
Identifiers: LCCN 2021027623 (print) | LCCN 2021027624 (ebook) | ISBN 9781564849199 (paperback) | ISBN 9781564848925 (epub) | ISBN 9781564849182 (pdf)
Subjects: LCSH: Maker movement in education. | Inclusive education. | Makerspaces.
Classification: LCC LB1029.M35 H34 2021 (print) | LCC LB1029.M35 (ebook) | DDC 371.33--dc23
LC record available at **https://lccn.loc.gov/2021027623**
LC ebook record available at **https://lccn.loc.gov/2021027624**

First Edition
ISBN: 978-1-56484-919-9

Ebook version available

Printed in the United States of America
ISTE® is a registered trademark of the International Society for Technology in Education.

About ISTE

The International Society for Technology in Education (ISTE) is home to a passionate community of global educators who believe in the power of technology to transform teaching and learning, accelerate innovation and solve tough problems in education.

ISTE inspires the creation of solutions and connections that improve opportunities for all learners by delivering: practical guidance, evidence-based professional learning, virtual networks, thought-provoking events and the ISTE Standards. ISTE is also the leading publisher of books focused on technology in education. For more information or to become an ISTE member, visit iste.org. Subscribe to ISTE's YouTube channel and connect with ISTE on Twitter, Facebook and LinkedIn.

Related ISTE Titles

Dive Into UDL: Immersive Practices to Develop Expert Learners
Kendra Grant and Luis Perez
iste.org/DiveIntoUDL

The New Assistive Tech: Make Learning Awesome for All!
Christopher R. Bugaj
iste.org/NewAssistiveTech

Inclusive Learning 365: Edtech Strategies for Every Day of the Year
Christopher R. Bugaj, Karen Janowski, Mike Marotta and Beth Poss
iste.org/Inclusive365

To see all books available from ISTE, please visit **iste.org/books**.

About the Author

CAROLINE HAEBIG has extensive experience designing and leading professional learning for teachers, instructional coaches, and administrators nationwide. Focused on helping educators develop innovative teaching, learning, and assessment practices, she has successfully facilitated student, teacher, and administrator preparation for school system 1:1 technology initiatives to support student learning and led district-wide work in the areas of inclusive maker learning as well as technological literacy. An accomplished educator, Haebig was named an ISTE Emerging Leader, Apple Distinguished Educator, Google Certified Innovator, and a recipient of the Wisconsin State Superintendent Service-Learning Award, the University of Indiana Jacobs Educator Award, and the ISTE Outstanding Young Educator award. When not working with education professionals, Haebig enjoys training for competitive cycling events, being active outdoors with friends and family, and spending time with her two Boston Terriers at home in Wisconsin.

Dedication

To my parents. I am forever grateful that my mother Elizabeth Haebig inspired and nurtured my passion and skills for engaging all learners in higher-order thinking and literacy from the very start of my career. My father Rene M. Haebig was a science educator by trade and a true maker and inventive problem solver in every way. His empathetic ability to connect with and help all types of people shaped my awareness of learner variability and compassion for others.

Acknowledgments

I'm very grateful to work with and be inspired by a variety of educators and champions of innovation and inclusion. Specifically, I'd like to thank: Cynthia Crannell for always demonstrating and stretching the possibilities of innovative maker work with the youngest of learners; Douglas Kiang for always being a sincere friend and colleague willing to lend a thoughtful ear and share meaningful feedback; Laura Schmidt for her steadfast efforts to bridge the work of education professionals and industry leaders in order to create powerful pathways that support learners and communities; Dr. Marguerite Sneed for her mentorship and editing skills over the years; and Dr. Susan Savaglio-Jarvis for coaching me professionally, sparking and supporting my passion for innovative teaching and learning from the start of my career.

This book also would not be possible without the support and expertise of Valerie Witte, Linda Laflamme, and Christopher G. Johnson. I am honored by the opportunity to learn from and with you.

Publisher's Acknowledgments

ISTE gratefully acknowledges the contributions of the following:

ISTE Standards reviewers

Veronica Baca

Heather White

Manuscript reviewers

Christopher Johnson

Montrey Peace

Contents

Introduction ... ix

Build an Inclusive Maker Learning Culture

View from the Field: Culture First, Tools Second ... 2

Maker Culture: Redefining Opportunities for Student Innovation ... 2

Define Maker Learning ... 10

Is It Making? ... 11

What Is Prototyping and Why Does It Matter? ... 16

Establish a Team of Maker Champions ... 22

Maker Manifesto ... 26

HOW-TO STRATEGIES:
Develop a Culture of Inclusive Maker Learning ... 28

Next Steps ... 36

Reflection ... 37

Develop a Systems-Based Approach to Inclusive Maker Learning

View from the Field: Embracing Diverse Perspectives ... 39

Connecting the Dots and Building Capacity ... 39

HOW-TO STRATEGIES:
Creating Breakthroughs ... 42

Next Steps	63
Reflection	63

Integrate UDL Guidelines Into Maker Experiences

View from the Field: Do We Need a Space for Making?	65
Creating Inclusive Spaces for Maker Learning	66
Steps to a High-Impact Virtual Makerspace	67
UDL in Your Maker Learning Environment	78
Next Steps	102
Reflection	102

Scaffolding the Student Design Process

Strategies for Each Phase of the Design Process	104
HOW-TO STRATEGIES:	
Unpacking the Design Challenge	106
Identifying a Target User or Audience	116
Research and Define	127
Defining Problems and Ideating Solutions	134
Sketching	144
Prototyping	151

Evaluation	161
Next Steps	167
Reflection	168

Expand Your Reach and Launch Maker Learning for All

View from the Field: Invest the Time	170
Build Understanding Across Stakeholder Groups	170
HOW-TO STRATEGIES: Spread the Word	172
Next Steps	183
Reflection	184

Continuous Improvement and Assessing Program Growth

View from the Field: What's the End Game?	186
Commit to Supporting Complex Change	187
Use Data to Make Informed Decisions and Evaluate Professional Learning	194
HOW-TO STRATEGIES: Evaluating Programmatic Growth	200
Micro-Credentials: Build Capacity Through Choice	207
Maker Roadmap: Guide the Journey	212
Next Steps and Reflection	215
References	217
Index	219

Introduction

Over the last year as I accompanied my mother to the hospital for numerous oncologist appointments, I couldn't help admiring its parking garage. Vibrant images of frogs, rainforest and frog sounds, consistent use of a bright yellow color, as well as text and braille signage all indicated the level we parked on and helped us navigate the space. As the year went on, we discovered each floor used unique themes, colors, and sounds—from ducks to storms—to help other visitors navigate the huge hospital complex.

Here, where I least expected it, was a powerful example of inclusive design. Information was provided so it could be perceived in multiple ways, preemptively removing barriers in the environment. It also was an example of an intentional design that was accessible and beneficial for more than those who are considered "average"—as nobody is precisely average.

School systems could learn a lot from that hospital parking garage. As they work to curate and create spaces and curriculum for making, whether physical and digital, they too should adopt an inclusive, accessible approach. Defined as a "design methodology that enables and draws on the full range of human diversity" (Microsoft, 2018), inclusive design looks for universal solutions that fit everybody. Too often this is overlooked. While I love the excitement and urgency around the value of maker learning, STEM, computational thinking, and innovative design, many education professionals jump to talking about such details as what spaces to build and which robots, tools, and materials to procure before defining their vision and purpose of maker learning. Without that vision, it's very hard to create a culture of maker learning, design thinking, and makerspaces that is accessible and inclusive for all learners.

That's where *The Maker Playbook* can help. Simply put, the goal of this book is to remove barriers and provide education professionals with concrete strategies for designing and implementing cultural and instructional supports for maker learning and equipping makerspaces—whether physical or digital—as well as to model the Universal Design for Learning Guidelines in action.

The strategies provided in this book are intended to help education professionals define maker learning and articulate the ideal outcomes of innovative learning experiences. These initial steps, along with identifying possible causes of exclusion, work to build a solid foundation for creating opportunities and environments that are accessible to all learners. They set the stage for school systems to develop spaces, procure resources, and create intentional learning experiences that eliminate barriers from the start. All learners need to have access to maker learning experiences that allow them to perceive information, interact with it, and make sense of it in a meaningful way. Because we want all learners to have this level of access, this book will address the value of digital creation and technologies as a valuable mechanism for creating pathways to accessible maker learning experiences.

The Foundation: Access and UDL

Underlying these steps and the book's philosophy are the Universal Design for Learning (UDL) Guidelines. Pioneered by the Center for Applied Special Technology (CAST) in the 1980s, the UDL Guidelines embody the years of research, collaborations, and identified best practices for guiding educators as they increase opportunities for all learners to access high-impact learning environments and experiences. Specifically, the UDL Guidelines provide direction on how to shape learning experiences and environments in ways that help *all* learners develop into expert learners. Expert learners are characterized as learners that are purposeful and motivated, resourceful and knowledgeable, strategic and goal directed (CAST, 2018).

UDL Guidelines

The Universal Design for Learning Guidelines were created to assist educators in developing flexible, accessible learning environments that address learner variability. Another significant goal of the UDL guidelines is to transition how educators focus their efforts from solely focusing on the specific or special needs of individuals in isolation, to increasing access to learning for all students in the environment.

The Access layer of the UDL Guidelines needs significant attention when exploring the context of maker learning and makerspaces. Unfortunately, many education professionals aren't thinking about accessibility as a basic entry point for addressing learner variability. Reflecting on my own experiences with UDL experts who have led workshops in my district's schools and walked teachers through unit design, I realized they spent very minimal time setting the stage for our work with accessibility. Sure, we reviewed what it could look like for educators to provide options for representing information, diversifying strategies to engage students in learning, and the importance of offering learner voice and choice.

Although we covered these important elements for addressing learner variability, we did not take the next steps. We did not spend the time to unpack the vital, first layer of the Universal Design for Learning Guidelines: Access. While CAST emphasizes that the UDL Guidelines are not prescriptive, the dimension of access is essential. Specifically, this means that barriers in the learning environment must be addressed prior to exploring the UDL Guidelines' next layers: Build and Internalize.

Consider Before You Design and Build

As Mischa Andrews wrote in her "Accessibility = Innovation" blog post, "In a perfect world accessibility would be embedded in the way we design and develop products; the way we make content; the way we think and talk about the spaces we live in" (2018). We have not reached that perfect world yet, but educators can take intentional steps toward it by slowing their rush to innovate and build the ultimate makerspace and, instead, giving accessibility the time and attention it deserves.

One powerful resource that you can use to help you think deeper when designing spaces and evaluating resources for maker learning is Inclusive: A Microsoft Design Toolkit. Specifically, the Toolkit's activity cards and support cards provide a variety of exercises that can push you to consider how different learners may experience possible maker environments, interactions with humans during the maker process, and objects provided to support making. When working as a team to make decisions about the organization of digital and physical spaces; the presentation of information; which tools, technologies, or resources to procure; or how to design sample learning experiences, for example, education professionals could use the activity cards to brainstorm and evaluate different scenarios and variables that may impact inclusivity and accessibility. Likewise, the Inclusive Toolkit's support cards are a great way to help you consider how different environments enable different capabilities or present limitations, which is particularly useful when brainstorming and evaluating specific elements of maker learning experiences and resources for making. Leveraging these tools can help you and your team better understand why and how students may be included or excluded from an experience and focus more on developing solutions to increase inclusion.

Makerspaces and design studios are different from typical classroom settings in that they offer more flexibility and resources for students to engage in the different stages of the design thinking process. Similarly, creating virtual makerspaces provides opportunities to scaffold how students engage in innovative design in remote learning environments. Because makerspaces are often a shared resource and available to all teachers and students in a school, they also provide an opportunity to model systematic techniques and strategies that teachers can transfer to their instructional practices and classrooms. By building specific supports into each makerspace, educators can capitalize on the ability of all students to grow as expert learners and innovative problem-solvers.

Who This Book Is For

Whether you work directly with students or are a school system leader, *The Maker Playbook* will assist you in taking a systems-based approach to democratizing how students gain access to unique tools and capacities for prototyping and testing authentic solutions. Whether you are a classroom teacher or a building or district administrator, this book provides ready-to-use strategies that use active learning techniques to engage participants. Specifically, these strategies and activities are intended to help participants visualize, evaluate, and create the necessary steps and resources for an inclusive maker and design culture.

If you're interested in how to create an inclusive maker culture at a systems level, you've come to the right place. Likewise, if you're looking for specific strategies you can use to develop an inclusive makerspace—physical or virtual, for young learners or adults—you'll find advice in these pages and projects to help you facilitate building and enhancing a maker learning culture. Whether your school system already has started this journey and is looking for ways to enhance established maker learning and makerspaces or is ready to start laying the foundation for providing maker learning experiences for all learners, the resources and strategies in this book are intended to democratize access to maker learning for all.

This book is also for educators who believe that all students can learn and for educators who take pride in developing the scaffolding to help all learners reach levels of higher-order thinking and engagement. In the chapters ahead, you'll find ready-to-use resources for guiding learners in the design thinking, maker learning process.

This book is intended to support you in your efforts to increase opportunities for all students to engage in maker learning and improve the accessibility of school makerspaces by incorporating resources and strategies that are derived from the Universal Design for Learning Guidelines.

What's in This Book

Educators are very busy people. The inspiration behind this book came from the desire to provide you with high-impact strategies you can put directly into action to foster an inclusive maker learning environment. At the online Introduction Resources page, you'll find **downloadable crosswalk tables** that list how the book's various strategies and resources align to the UDL Guidelines and ISTE Standards for Students and Standards for Educators (simply scan the QR code at the end of this Introduction).

Navigating the Strategies

In each chapter, you'll find specific strategies that facilitate the collaborative approach needed to design a high-impact, inclusive maker learning culture, physical or virtual makerspace. To help you get started quickly, each strategy outlines the essentials:

- Duration of the activity
- Recommended number of people
- What you'll need
- The goal or purpose of the activity
- When to use it
- What to do

Plus, each strategy includes a list of the ISTE Standards that it aligns with.

You can implement all the strategies and techniques in this book in an in-person or remote learning setting. Although the main how-to steps for each strategy are written as if participants are together in person, the "Go Remote" sidebars that accompany them will help you adapt the learning to a virtual setting. In addition, the elements and techniques shared in these sidebars offer opportunities to improve the accessibility of collaborative in-person work. Because many of the techniques follow similar themes, such as brainstorming and refining ideas, sorting and voting on solutions and ideas, and documenting the process and progress of your work, the Introduction Resources page provides a roundup of frequently used tools and tips to help you make the most of digital tools no matter the environment; scan the QR code and look for the **Go Remote: Tools & Techniques to Support Collaboration Everywhere** document.

Because you don't have a lot of time to re-create or replicate specific resources, each chapter ends with a QR code that links to shortcuts to help you jump into action. Scan the code to find digital versions of the graphic organizers and templates used in the strategies, as well as links to tools and websites mentioned in the chapter. Use this book as an active learning resource.

Playbook Signs and Signals

The strategies and resources presented in *The Maker Playbook* will assist you in several aspects of your work. To help you identify which to use at what stage of the game, watch for the following signs and signals:

 CREATING AN INCLUSIVE VISION

These strategies help you to:

- Visualize inclusive maker learning
- Develop and implement an authentic definition of inclusive maker learning
- Articulate connections between student learning goals and engaging learners in a deliberate design process
- Identify essential qualities and characteristics learners should experience during maker and design work

 BUILDING EDUCATOR SKILLS

These are tools to:

- Identify and evaluate specific skills educators need to create inclusive maker environments
- Monitor new skill development and identify new needs and next steps

IDENTIFYING INCENTIVES

These help you create opportunities for:

- Entry points into inclusive maker learning experiences that engage the interests of all stakeholders
- Stakeholders to act strategically

PROCURING RESOURCES

These help you identify:

- Resources (physical, time, social, or human) that sustain effort and motivation while building an inclusive maker learning culture
- Methods for introducing resources in ways that help stakeholders perceive the opportunities these resources bring to all learners
- Opportunities to assist how educators and learners physically respond in the makerspace or with maker resources

PARTICIPATING IN ONGOING ACTION PLANNING

These help you organize:

- Action steps for stakeholder groups
- A timeline of work to ensure all stakeholders receive appropriate learning, training, and practice
- Opportunities for ongoing progress monitoring and providing mastery-oriented feedback to stakeholders at various points in your process

Tips for Getting Started

Introduction Resources

When embarking on any new project, the excitement to begin may be laced with a bit of trepidation: There's so much to learn, so many possible strategies. How do you decide where to begin or identify the most effective ideas to try? Before you turn the page, here are a few tips that will help you get the most out of what you find there:

- Be open to rethinking what it means to increase participation and ways for all learners to access maker learning experiences and environments.
- Think big, start small. Identify one specific outcome you want to focus on and start with one strategy.
- Define opportunities in your curriculum to use maker learning and innovative design to engage learners in authentic problem-solving.
- Consider how scaffolding the steps of the design process increases the opportunities for all learners to thrive.
- Reflect on how the strategies included in this book also model the principles of Universal Design for Learning for adult learners.

Build an Inclusive Maker Learning Culture

By the end of this chapter, you will:

- Gain actionable steps you can take to begin creating an inclusive culture of maker learning

- Differentiate between technological literacy and educational technology

- Assess how the Computational Thinker and Innovative Designer ISTE Standards for Students are valuable for creating and guiding student maker learning experiences

- Evaluate a variety of methods that can be used to develop a definition of inclusive maker learning, write a maker manifesto, and devise a team of maker champions

View from the Field: Culture First, Tools Second

In my work with maker learning, design thinking, and developing makerspaces across a PK–12 school system, I see many educators working to redefine the skills, knowledge, and dispositions students will need to develop to be successful in a rapidly, technologically evolving world. I hear lots of conversations on how to increase opportunities for students to grow as innovative problem solvers with a technological edge. Unfortunately, all too often I also see school leaders rush toward innovation by building makerspaces or purchasing consumable materials, robots, and 3D printers without first defining what high-impact maker learning is. Further, I see school systems often skip the part of defining what the term *maker* means within the context of the other work they are doing. They're going about the process backwards. To create high-impact uses of any resources, educational leaders need to focus on first building an inclusive culture of maker learning that centers on inventive problem-solving.

This chapter explores key concepts and strategies that will help you get started in developing an inclusive culture of maker learning—whether you come from the perspective of a school district, building, or classroom.

Maker Culture: Redefining Opportunities for Student Innovation

In order to develop an inclusive, high-impact maker learning culture at the school-system level, you need to define what maker learning means within your organization's strategic goals and culture. To do that effectively, however, you first need to understand how maker learning provides an avenue to developing literacies that can improve student readiness for college, careers, and life.

Literacies for Success

In his book *Robot-Proof: Higher Education in the Age of Artificial Intelligence*, Joseph E. Aoun defined and focused on three literacies that he believed would be most crucial to help current students and workers be successful in an age of rapid technological advancement and artificial intelligence: technological literacy, data literacy, and human literacy (2017). In short, *technological literacy* is the ability to understand how current and emerging technologies are impacting industry practices and how people live. The smart technologies of today gather more data than ever before, and *data literacy* skills enable us to analyze and leverage this data in meaningful ways. Once data analysis is achieved, we use *human literacy* to discover new ways to improve the human experience with meaningful applications of this data (Aoun, 2017).

Technological literacy is more than simply using instructional and educational technology, however. Instructional technology offers powerful opportunities for students to demonstrate creativity, engage in collaboration, and support modes for communication for the purpose of learning. Using these tools strictly for improving workflow and increasing options for students to have voice and choice in how they express learning does not necessarily translate into students being technologically literate.

What skills do you feel are necessary for all students to develop?

Maker learning experiences guided by the design thinking process offer opportunities to develop a variety of learners' technological literacy skills and engage them in authentic problem-solving experiences that can relate to a wide range of curricula. Developing a maker *culture* provides a vehicle for students to develop technological literacy as it relates to specific aspects of their curriculum. Simply opening a makerspace for students to use the tools it contains is not enough. Educators must be able to identify how the curriculum can be the vehicle for students to engage in design thinking and develop appropriate technological literacy skills. Having a maker learning process rooted in design thinking provides an opportunity for students to define specific problems and create and test prototypes of authentic solutions. Furthermore, the design thinking process provides an avenue for learners to also develop technological, data, and human literacy skills.

Connecting the ISTE Standards for Students

The ISTE Standards for Students are a great place to start thinking about the specific types of skills, knowledge, and dispositions that students need to develop to be successful in today and tomorrow's world. They also offer a powerful starting place from which to define an inclusive maker learning environment. While maker learning experiences have the potential to engage learners in all the ISTE Standards for Students, homing in on the Innovative Designer and Computational Thinker standards offers a way to highlight how maker learning and makerspaces provide an opportunity to develop technological literacy skills while adding value to curriculum. These two standards capture skills and dispositions that uphold the principles of UDL. For example, authenticity is a driving component of the Action and Expression principle of the Universal Design for Learning Guidelines (CAST, 2018), and the Innovative Designer and Computational Thinker standards encourage the practices of student-centered inquiry and the creation of authentic products. In addition, these standards promote additional skills that lay a foundation for preparing learners for the impact of the rapid acceleration of technology, boosting their technological literacy.

INNOVATIVE DESIGNER STANDARD

The Innovative Designer standard (ISTE, 2016) provides a roadmap for educators to create opportunities for students to act strategically, express themselves fluently, and physically respond. To help you get started on this journey, let's take a look at each objective of the Innovative Designer standard paired with some entry points you can try:

4a. Students know and use a deliberate design process for generating ideas, testing theories, creating innovative artifacts or solving authentic problems.

- Provide an overview of the steps of the design process, and review why the process is valuable and when to use it.
- Provide a dedicated time for brainstorming, and model brainstorming techniques learners can use and norms they should follow.
- Have students explore real-world examples of the design process and how it is used to solve problems in a variety of industries.
- Engage students in exercises of games such as Disruptus, MockUps, or Extraordinaires to get them thinking creatively about design and problem-solving.
- Create activities where students are required to empathize with a specific audience in order to solve a problem.

4b. Students select and use digital tools to plan and manage a design process that considers design constraints and calculated risks.

- Provide students with a timeline for the project and include specific checkpoints for formative feedback and review.
- Use graphic organizers to help students collect and visualize data they are collecting through the interview and observation or prototyping process.
- Encourage students to create visualizations of their data using graphic design tools, spreadsheets, or video creation tools.
- Create scaffolded opportunities for students to analyze their data and decide on next steps. Sentence stems and prompts offer a way for students to dive deeper into the data they are analyzing, for example: *I see..., I think..., I find..., I will..., Next we can try..., I wonder...,* and so on.
- Have students create websites where they use a variety of mediums to share the progress of their work and reflections at specific stages of the design process.

4c. Students develop, test and refine prototypes as part of a cyclical design process.

- Work with students to unpack the purpose that prototypes serve in the design process.
- Familiarize students with common vocabulary of the prototyping process.
- Provide students with examples of the different types of prototypes that exist, such as paper, digital, native, and so on.
- Require students to sketch their prototypes before making them.
- Develop opportunities for students to understand what resources are available for making various prototypes.
- Provide students with a prototyping checklist that they can use as they test their prototypes.
- Create opportunities for students to explain how their prototype works.

4d. Students exhibit a tolerance for ambiguity, perseverance and the capacity to work with open-ended problems.

- Provide learners with a clear, specific challenge or problem they are solving.
- Use a variety of multimedia to introduce learners to the challenge and to build background knowledge.
- Develop content area vocabulary in addition to design process vocabulary when kicking off the design challenge.
- Take the time to help learners understand the different parts of the design process in relation to the design challenge or problem.
- Break the research process into digestible chunks and work with students to develop questions that will guide their research.
- Provide students with graphic organizers to track the information they are collecting, or increase opportunities for student choice and invite students to create their own graphic organizers or sketchnotes.

In the chapters that follow, we'll delve deeper into many of these suggestions and you'll find resources and templates to help you.

COMPUTATIONAL THINKER STANDARD

The Computational Thinker standard (ISTE, 2016) supports educators in their efforts to create opportunities for students to hone their problem-solving skills while also increasing their technical literacy. To help you leverage this standard, let's take a look at each objective of the Computational Thinker standard paired with some entry points you can try:

5a. *Students formulate problem definitions suited for technology-assisted methods such as data analysis, abstract models and algorithmic thinking in exploring and finding solutions.*

- Provide learners with real-world examples of technology-assisted methods for data analysis, abstract models, and algorithmic thinking for exploring and finding solutions.
- Develop opportunities for learners to practice reviewing data sets and identifying trends they notice.
- Develop opportunities for learners to clearly define the problem they are exploring based on data analysis.
- Provide experiences for learners to develop basic computational thinking skills. These can range from block coding to no-tech activities.
- Use block coding tools to allow learners to make and test predictions.

5b. *Students collect data or identify relevant data sets, use digital tools to analyze them, and represent data in various ways to facilitate problem-solving and decision-making.*

- Use learner-created problem statements and hypotheses to guide learners as they explore data sets.
- Develop opportunities for learners to use digital tools to collect data sets. Some practical starting points may include using scientific tools, or even something as simple as Google Forms, to create surveys or enter observational or interview data.
- Provide opportunities for learners to analyze real-world data sets. Some sources include Google Trends (curated by Google), Global Health Observatory Data (curated by the World Health Organization), Earthdata (curated by NASA), Pew Internet (curated by the Pew Research Center), and Data.gov.sg (curated by the Singaporean government).

- Develop opportunities for learners to use infographic creation tools to represent data in various forms.

- Have learners create reflections and summaries that reflect key takeaways and next-step decisions they will make based on the data sets they analyzed.

5c. Students break problems into component parts, extract key information, and develop descriptive models to understand complex systems or facilitate problem-solving.

- Provide learners with graphic organizers to scaffold how they break problems into parts.

- Use graphic design tools to have learners create their own visual representations of problems they have identified and the key information they want to focus on.

- Develop opportunities for learners to use 3D design software to create and test solutions to problems they are solving.

- Use simulation tools, such as those available at **phet.colorado.edu**, to ease how learners collect data, extracting key information to develop understanding of complex systems and concepts.

- Provide opportunities to have students sort data into specific descriptive categories based on data trends and make predictions based on their findings.

5d. Students understand how automation works and use algorithmic thinking to develop a sequence of steps to create and test automated solutions.

- Develop opportunities for learners to make connections between course content and real-world connections to automation in various industries and careers.

- Provide learners with programming and robotics challenges where they must document their steps and test solutions.

- Develop preliminary algorithmic thinking skills by having learners use a daily process (like making a peanut butter and jelly sandwich, or checking out a library book) by creating and following a set of step-by-step instructions to complete a task and discuss what would happen if these steps were not followed.

- Have learners use flowcharts to model a process.

- Provide opportunities for learners to create 3D models, blueprints, and data models to build conceptual models and set a relationship between data and solve a problem. (You can view sample lesson plans at **equip.learning.com**.)

We'll delve deeper into different aspects of computational thinking in chapters to follow. For now, keep in mind that computational thinking and skills can be developed throughout various stages of the design process. Furthermore, computational thinking skills provide learners with a solid foundation for diving deeper into problem-solving, coding, exploring innovative uses of technology, and fostering creativity.

SUPPORT SKILL BUILDING

When it comes to these standards, we must remember that these skills can be developed in high-, low-, or even no-tech ways. This is important to keep in mind while developing a definition and culture of maker learning. All students can develop design skills and reach standards if we are providing diverse means, tools, and capacities to do so.

What do you *know* about high- and low-tech ways to develop computational thinking and design skills?

STOP & JOT

What do you *want to know* about high- and low-tech ways to develop computational thinking and design skills?

We cannot expect students to develop authentic solutions that incorporate computational thinking, coding, or programming if they are not exposed to opportunities to develop the computational thinking skills first. It is well worth the time to incorporate skill-builder activities during which learners are introduced to coding and then can develop algorithmic thinking or various methods for collecting and visualizing data. When educators provide learners with the opportunity to develop these skills, even in isolation initially, then learners are more likely to be able to incorporate and apply these skills and methods to the solutions they develop and prototypes they make.

Define Maker Learning

Taking the time to develop an authentic definition of maker learning is an important step to designing inclusive maker experiences and resources. Having a definition of maker learning is valuable because it can also be used as a tool to guide educators and students in the ongoing development and growth of maker learning within your school culture. Whether you are a classroom educator working directly with students or leading a school system, defining maker learning is a powerful step toward developing understanding and outlining next steps for those engaged in the work. In addition to using a definition of making to build a foundation, actively using an authentic definition of making or maker learning can facilitate the evolving growth and continuous improvement of your program as well. Although individual teachers can define the term for their own classroom environments or personal maker activities, crafting a definition at the district or school level is more powerful and creates a systematic impact.

So, what *is* the definition of maker learning? There is no single, right answer, but consider an example:

> *Maker Learning in our school system offers opportunities for all students to ask questions, seek solutions, and build and represent their ideas using unique tools and capacities. Throughout the process of "making" and design thinking, learners access tools and techniques that allow them to design, prototype, evaluate, and reflect. Making is connected to curriculum-based learning and passion-based learning.*

As you work through the brainstorming prompts and strategies in this chapter to devise your own authentic definition of maker learning, continually question how that evolving definition may include or exclude students. It is especially important to be mindful of how specific experiences or environmental factors may create unintentional barriers. Taking the time to create a student empathy canvas that represents the different senses can be useful for determining if a specific sense is needed to be successful and what can be done to prevent situational limitations.

Is It Making?

To help educators in your district deepen their understanding of inclusive maker learning, engage them in the Is It Making activity, which challenges participants to identify scenarios that represent key elements for a definition of maker learning. This activity is exceptionally useful in helping educators differentiate maker learning that incorporates specific skills outlined by the Innovative Designer and Computational Thinker ISTE Student Standards from other project-based tasks that don't require students to develop authentic solutions. The key is to get educators to differentiate how a maker challenge would require students to define specific problems and make and test their prototypes. In addition, this activity is very helpful for assisting teachers in visualizing how maker learning could fit within their curriculum.

To prepare participants, first unpack the Innovative Designer and Computational Thinker standards and share what your school system has identified as core elements of maker learning. This is valuable for helping educators discriminate between the different scenarios. When educators in my district participated in the Is It Making activity, we watched for three indicators of maker learning when evaluating the scenarios:

- **THE PRESENCE OF THE 3 As:** *Agency* (kids decide on the pathway to product/solution/invention), *Authenticity* (students are making with a purpose and meaning), and *Audience* (learners design, create, and invent for humans). This indicator helped educators understand the importance of student voice and choice in developing authentic solutions for a specific intended audience, rather than telling students what to create.

- **COMPONENTS OF THE DESIGN THINKING PROCESS:** A focus on a design approach, rooted in empathy, ideation, prototyping, testing, and iteration that favors inventive thinking. This indicator guided educators in creating learning experiences that developed specific student skills unique to the Innovative Designer standard. Including this direction also helped educators better understand what it means to have students make and test prototypes.

- **UNIQUE TOOLS AND CAPACITIES:** Access to and use of unique maker tools that present students with different options to make. This indicator encouraged educators to consider how student prototypes can be developed using high- and low-tech materials. This indicator also opened doors to having conversations about dedicating a specific space and resources to making and design processes.

Is It Making? Sample Prompts

To help you get started with the Is It Making activity, here are some prompts that you can use, along with explanations of how they stack up compared to the example definition of maker learning. Do they qualify as "making" based on your school's definition?

SCENARIO 1

The fourth grade class is studying erosion. The teacher asks students to use a pan and some sand to demonstrate how erosion works.

ANSWER: Not making, according to the example definition. Students aren't deciding on the solution and aren't provided with an opportunity to solve a problem.

ADJUSTED CHALLENGE: Explore how erosion impacts habitats of animals or lives of people. Develop a solution that addresses a specific problem that erosion brings to people's lives.

SCENARIO 2

The teacher instructs students in a middle school Spanish class to create a website that increases Spanish-speaking citizens' awareness about health services in the city of Milwaukee.

ANSWER: Not making, according to the example definition. While this challenge does identify a specific audience, student authenticity can be increased by allowing students to decide on a product that they will be making to meet the need of the target audience.

ADJUSTED CHALLENGE: How would you increase awareness about health services for Latino populations in the city of Milwaukee?

SCENARIO 3

Their teacher tells first-grade students to create a representation of the water cycle using rapid prototyping materials.

ANSWER: This one is tricky. While the activity may serve as a useful skill builder to learn about the water cycle, it does not require students to dig into a problem related to the water cycle or to develop their own solution.

ADJUSTED CHALLENGE: Create a representation of the cycle to teach your friend about how the cycle works. Alternatively, develop a solution to an issue that is related to the water cycle.

SCENARIO 4

High school advanced placement psychology students must complete one of three challenge options: Develop a way to explain an abstract concept to someone with little understanding. Or, develop a way to explain neurotransmission to someone; be sure to identify who your target audience is and why they would need to know about it. Or, develop a way to explain Alzheimer's Disease to a family member of a patient.

ANSWER: Yes, this is making. These scenarios all require students to apply their knowledge of learning as well as structures and functions of the brain to teach an abstract concept to a specific audience. Students choose their own solution, identifying a target audience and incorporating an empathetic connection.

CUSTOMIZE CHALLENGES

Whether evaluating scenarios such as these or designing maker opportunities in your school, remember that educators know their learners best and should consider the unique needs and developmental appropriateness of the challenges they are creating. Some students will need more direction and specificity in the challenge than others. Overall, it is best to help educators understand how the student experience is impacted by the challenge. Teachers must create maker challenges that provide learners with the opportunity to explore a problem and develop and test a prototype of their authentic solution.

Focus On the Why

To assist educators in identifying opportunities for authentic, maker learning in their curriculum and more easily answer the *Is it making?* question, ask them to consider how they would explain to a student *why* the content or skills they are learning are valuable and applicable to lifelong learning. Unpacking the why frequently leads educators to articulate the real-world applications and connections to the content they are teaching, and this leads to real-world problems that students can research and then present ideas of possible solutions to.

In other words, consider the whole picture of the design process, rather than focusing on only *what* students are being told to do or make. Facilitate educators in crafting challenges for which students define problems, observe, research, collect data, and then develop and test authentic solutions. Specifically, the dynamic between educators and learners during the process of making should support how students are able to answer the questions of what, why, and for whom they are making.

Increase the Clarity of Your Maker Challenge

Another approach that is helpful when crafting student challenges is to follow the elements of GRASPS (Goal, Role, Audience, Situation, Purpose, Standards) as outlined by Grant Wiggins and Jay McTighe in *The Understanding by Design Guide to Advanced Concepts in Creating and Reviewing Units* (2012). Connecting the elements of GRASPS to the outline of a typical design brief bridges the gap between using student-friendly language and best instructional practice with the core components used by industry. Consider how the sentence starters and indicators in Table 1.1 (adapted from Wiggins & McTighe, 2012) can help you ideate ways to improve teacher clarity when constructing and communicating a maker learning challenge.

TABLE 1.1 Crafting a Maker Design Challenge with GRASPS

ELEMENT	SENTENCE STARTERS AND INDICATORS
Goal	• Your task is: • Your goal is to… • The problem is… • Your challenge is… • The obstacles to overcome are… • The project is about, and the purpose is to…
Role	• You are… • Your job is… • You are asked to…
Audience	• The target audience for the solution you develop is: • Your clients are: • Stakeholders in this work include… • You need to convince… • Things to identify or note about your target audience: demographics, needs, pain points, hobbies, mindset (Depending on your challenge, students may also be the ones to identify their target audience.)
Situation	• Your constraints are… • The challenge involves facing…. • The budget or limitations are… • Materials you have available for this work include….

ELEMENT	SENTENCE STARTERS AND INDICATORS
Purpose	• Make a prototype that demonstrates your solution. • Make a prototype that communicates... • Develop a solution that...
Standards and Criteria for Success	• Project milestones are... • The project timeline is... • Qualities of deliverables include... • Your product must meet the following criteria... • Your work will be evaluated on the following... • A successful solution and prototype will include... • What good looks like...

What Is Prototyping and Why Does It Matter?

Once teachers develop high-impact maker challenges for students that incorporate authentic research and problem-solving strategies, the next place they often get stuck is with the concept of *prototyping*. I've heard educators claim that having students write multiple drafts of a paper or create teacher-directed dioramas is "prototyping" (it's not) or because "my students really aren't going to make a real..." prototyping isn't important (it is). These educators are mistakenly focusing on or prescribing the end product learners are making. What matters most and should be their focus, however, is what the learner is doing to define and research a problem, identify a possible solution, and make and test a prototype, a model of their solution. Sketching is a powerful way to help learners conceptualize this process before making their first prototype.

The focus on student choice is an integral part of an authentic design process, and an authentic design process is integral to developing skills students need to succeed in their futures. Learners should be able to explain how their prototype works and how they will test it, collect data, and iterate. The Universal Design for Learning principles and the ISTE Standards for Students back this up. The UDL Action & Expression guidelines and checkpoints highlight the importance of providing learners with opportunities to choose how they will demonstrate learning (CAST, 2018). Similarly, the Innovative Designer standard recommends students "know and use a deliberate design process for generating ideas, testing theories, creating innovative artifacts or solving authentic problems" and "develop, test and refine prototypes as part of a cyclical design process" (indicators 4a and 4c, ISTE, 2016).

Prototypes Don't Have to Be Perfect

Educators often grapple with the idea that students will be developing detailed sketches and solutions during prototyping, but the actual making of their work would come in the form of found materials, low-resolution 3D printing, paper, or a digital tool modeling a virtual version of an end product. The juxtaposition of precision planning with a rough mock-up, however, is not as unusual as they might think. Sharing examples of the diverse ways prototypes can look based on the phase of prototype development or across different industries can be eye-opening. For instance, some powerful industry examples include:

- Paper prototypes and wireframes that demonstrate how an app for a smartphone would work
- Rapid prototypes of medical equipment made from found materials in a conference room
- Cardboard prototypes to test the impact of different counter heights on the customer experience at restaurants or hotels
- High-fidelity digital and native prototypes that involve coding to create a website

When educators can see that prototypes don't have to be highly technical in nature or high-resolution to be effective, they also can gain a deeper understanding of the value that the prototyping process provides students. Prototyping is building to think and provides a way to share student thinking.

In his book *Change by Design* (2009), Tim Brown emphasized the value of creating a design thinking culture, stating that design thinking is not just for designers. Brown also stressed the value of using fast and cheap prototyping methods as a way to generate timely results that allow for more time to be allocated to refining larger ideas. While aimed at Brown's business audience, this philosophy is a powerful reminder for educators, too: Prototypes don't have to be perfect or ready for real use in order to be effective (Figure 1.1). Because prototypes are intended to visualize ideas, provide opportunities to explain how possible solutions work, and encourage constructive feedback, they also provide a process that can be inherently flexible and inclusive. In addition, the prototyping process provides opportunities to engage learners in mastery-oriented, real-time feedback.

Figure 1.1 Low-resolution, rapid prototyping using paper or found materials is a powerful way to visualize ideas and gather feedback quickly.

PROTOTYPING FAQS

WHAT QUALITY SHOULD PROTOTYPES BE?

- Early prototypes should be fast, rough, and cheap.
- Rapid prototypes give form to ideas.

WHAT VALUE SHOULD PROTOTYPING BRING TO A PROJECT?

- Prototyping generates faster results to the overall solution development.
- Prototyping provides students the opportunity to creatively demonstrate their ideas using unique tools and capacities.
- Prototyping as a process provides opportunities to incorporate ongoing self-reflection and peer feedback to the maker learning process.

WHY IS STUDENT PROTOTYPE TESTING IMPORTANT?

- Prototypes must be able to be tested and evaluated, and help refine larger ideas.
- Students can develop skills necessary to collect, visualize, and analyze data.

Visualize It: Prototyping Videos

Inspiration comes at the strangest time. While I was doing dishes and listening to music via YouTube, I saw a commercial that was a great picture of maker learning. I knew I had to show it to my teachers to help them visualize the ISTE Standards for Students and maker learning in action. It worked, and the more I looked, the more commercials and short videos I found that captured specific skills of the design thinking process in action. Table 1.2 details seven of my favorites, but don't limit yourself to these. Look for other video clips or commercials that capture the core values of inclusive maker learning that you have outlined in your maker learning definition. When you share them with your fellow educators, be sure to point out the video or commercial's intended audience so participants don't get stuck on the commercial's persuasive aspects. Instead, have teachers identify the skills, knowledge, or dispositions that depict maker learning

TABLE 1.2 Short Videos to Help Visualize Maker Learning

VIDEO	POWERFUL FOR VISUALIZING	PROMPTS TO CONSIDER WHILE WATCHING	WHY THIS VIDEO?
Meet Molly, the Kid Who Never Stops Inventing GE Commercial bit.ly/2RKBAQd	• Expert learners • Maker skills • Knowledge • Dispositions	• What do you see? • What's interesting? • What skills does she exhibit?	Excellent for visualizing the core elements of what it means to be an expert learner. Molly is purposeful, motivated, resourceful, knowledgeable, strategic, and goal-directed. The video captures the specific skills and actions students take during the design process: sketching, testing, using materials for alternative uses, thinking outside the box, programming and mechanics, and problem-solving.

continues

CHAPTER 1: BUILD AN INCLUSIVE MAKER LEARNING CULTURE

VIDEO	POWERFUL FOR VISUALIZING	PROMPTS TO CONSIDER WHILE WATCHING	WHY THIS VIDEO?
Everyone Can Code—Apple WWDC 2016 bit.ly/3oXQLS9	• Finding empathetic connections • Problem-solving • Design thinking process	• What do all these app developers have in common (besides swift coding)?	Does a wonderful job showing how app developers create an app incrementally. They start with coding very basic things like a bouncing ball or a to-do list. The video also points out the value of planning, having an intended audience, and creating something that is rooted in empathy or improving people's lives.
How to Make a Cardboard Prototype bit.ly/3i04Xsh	• Value of prototypes	• Make an inference about what prototyping is.	Provides a clear overview of the steps that take place during the development of prototypes. This video brings clarity to why prototyping is useful as a part of the design process, provides clear examples for how rapid prototyping materials such as cardboard are valuable, and highlights the role that testing plays in prototype refinement.
*Rapid Prototyping: Sketching	Google for Startups* bit.ly/3fW4e8M	• Identifying different types of prototyping methods	• What are three Main Ideas, two I Wonder questions, and one Connection?	Provides clear examples of real-world industry uses of prototyping, and also differentiates between sketching, paper, and rapid prototyping, with digital prototyping and native prototyping. It is powerful for educators to be able to differentiate between the types of prototyping methods and to evaluate which method is most appropriate for their students. It is exceptionally important for educators to see how sketching and paper prototyping play very valuable roles within industry. Rapid prototyping materials are real, powerful, and aren't just for young people.

WHAT IS PROTOTYPING AND WHY DOES IT MATTER?

VIDEO	POWERFUL FOR VISUALIZING	PROMPTS TO CONSIDER WHILE WATCHING	WHY THIS VIDEO?
Apple Round Pizza Box Ad—Apple at Work—The Underdogs bit.ly/3c1nmkG	• Design thinking process	• Which elements of the design thinking process do you see?	Showcases all the elements that go into the design thinking process—from market research to sketching to prototyping to 3D printing to pitching the final work. This video is a delightful way to connect learners and educators to all the different steps of design thinking.
Not Everything Makes the Cut bit.ly/3hXcOly	• Prototype testing	• What can you infer about prototype testing?	High-impact when it comes to focusing on the importance of testing prototypes. Beyond its star-filled comedy, this ad for Amazon Alexa also highlights that not all solutions are viable, and that's why testing prototypes is just as important as making them.
ISTE Innovative Designer Playlist bit.ly/3c3gFhZ	• Innovative Designer standard in action • Gaining educator perspective • Viewing samples of student work	• What components of the Innovative Designer standard are you familiar with? • What is something that is new to you? • What is a possible starting point for integrating the objectives of the Innovative Designer standard in new ways?	Provides powerful examples and educator insights about the ways various content areas provide opportunities to engage in the design process. Each video in the playlist focuses on one of the four indicators for the Innovative Designer standard.

Establish a Team of Maker Champions

Developing a culture of maker learning for all begins with building the capacity of educators to understand what maker learning is and why it provides students with skills that are necessary and different from other teaching and learning methods. It is important for educators to experience maker learning firsthand and explore the design process with their students. Engaging educators in these firsthand learning experiences also provides an opportunity to consider how a specific learning experience, technology, or set of materials can be presented or modified to offer the most accessible environment or experience as possible. With its activity cards and prompts, Inclusive: A Microsoft Design Toolkit (**microsoft.com/design/inclusive**), can help guide you and your team in the reflection process after a specific learning experience. For example, the Mismatch to Solution I and II activity card can help participants unpack an experience through the lens of making it more accessible. The guiding questions provided in these activities are powerful: How might we create…? How might we improve…? How might we enable…?

Ideally, this exploration should occur as part of a team of early adopters; in my district we called them Maker Champion Teacher Leaders. This cohort of Maker Champions works together to explore the potential of maker learning with support from members of school leadership and those leading and supporting this work. Starting with a smaller group of educators who are willing to explore, grapple with ideas, and test out practices is highly advantageous before whole-system implementation. Tasked with a three-year arc of goals, the Maker Champions cohort works in its first year to establish a clear definition of maker learning and develop an implementation plan for inclusive learning through making. In its second, the cohort assesses progress and makes recommendations for scaling up maker learning across the system as well as for procuring necessary resources. In the third year, Maker Champions look both back and forwards, assessing progress so far, as well as building full-scale implementation of maker learning practices and identifying programmatic next steps for rolling out the what, the how, and where maker learning fits within the larger-scale curriculum and instructional practices. The "Sample Recruiting Document" sidebar provides an example communication for the Maker Champions cohort selection process and a more thorough timeline. (Scan the chapter's QR code for a downloadable and customizable version of the document.)

ESTABLISH A TEAM OF MAKER CHAMPIONS

If a school system is looking to create systemic change, structures need to be in place to adequately support these efforts. Appropriate planning and coordinating will provide opportunities to explore opportunities for release time, professional learning, mentoring, and learning by doing.

> **STOP & JOT**
>
> **List characteristics of your ideal team of Maker Champions.**

SAMPLE RECRUITING DOCUMENT

MAKER CHAMPIONS COHORT

The *[insert school system/district/school name]* is building a culture of making. Specifically, maker learning provides unique opportunities for students to achieve the vision of our graduate.

Maker Champion teachers are invited to work alongside district and building leadership to participate in the process of defining and illustrating what high-impact, inclusive maker learning looks like in our school system.

MAKER CHAMPIONS

Developing a culture of maker learning begins with building the ability of educators to understand the impact of student learning experiences designed around a maker learning and design process. To begin building this capacity, it is important for educators to experience authentic maker learning and have the opportunities to explore the process with their students. In the *[insert school system/district/school name]*, this exploration should occur as part of a team that works together to explore the potential of maker learning with support from members of the group's leadership team. We see participation on this cohort as defined by a teacher who is already engaging students in design thinking and maker learning, and is willing to:

- Advocate for maker learning, for student makers, and the development of a maker disposition in students
- Actively seek opportunities to learn about maker learning either independently or with others
- Actively seek opportunities to provide maker learning opportunities for their students

ESTABLISH A TEAM OF MAKER CHAMPIONS

- Engage in strategic risk-taking and engage in prototyping new making experiences with students
- Work as a participatory member of a collaborative team
- Communicate with other teachers, members of the collaborative team, and their school community about maker learning

A Maker Champion:

- Develops the skills and dispositions of a maker
- Develops an understanding of what maker learning means in your system and how making impacts teaching and learning in the district or school system
- Establishes connections between maker learning and curriculum, instruction, and assessment *(Where are potential integration points? Where are opportunities to design new experiences?)*
- Plans, implements, and assesses maker learning experiences
- Contributes findings, results, and insights associated with beta maker learning projects (with support from *[insert your own ideal role-player or department info]* as a partner in the documentation)
- Serves as an advocate for making in *[insert school system/district/school name]*

Being a Maker Champion is an opportunity to:

- Serve as a teacher-leader
- Advance the conditions for innovative teaching and learning practices
- Engage in professional learning around making and grow as a professional
- Work closely with other colleagues and other leaders as a collaborative team

continues

> **SAMPLE RECRUITING DOCUMENT continued**
>
> ### OVERVIEW OF TIMELINES FOR MAKER CHAMPION WORK AND PROGRAMMATIC ASSESSMENT AND GROWTH
>
> **PREPARATION:** Participate in professional learning prior to the start of the school year.
>
> **YEAR ONE:** Engage in new learning around what maker learning is and identify curriculum entry points for maker learning, developing skills and activities that support the curriculum. Provide input into procurement of tools and supplies, developing assessments for maker opportunities and providing insights on the development of an assessment process for the program. The product of the work during this year is to develop an implementation plan for learning through making.
>
> **YEAR TWO:** Review previous year's assessment and continued implementation of Maker Champion Plans and program evaluation. Make recommendations for moving to scale across the system that are created with support from the Maker Champions. Identify and procure resources for maker learning (makerspaces/materials/etc.).
>
> **YEAR THREE:** Review Year One and Two assessment and strategic full-scale implementation of maker learning practices, makerspaces/resources, and ongoing assessment for programmatic next steps.

Maker Manifesto

In addition to crafting a definition of maker learning, you and your Maker Champion Cohort need to further develop and illustrate what maker learning looks like in action. Creating a Maker Manifesto provides a way to deepen understanding and develop specific maker behaviors and mindsets. Containing specifics or examples of what maker learning looks like in action, a Maker Manifesto is a way to further clarify what maker learning would feel and look like if someone walked into a classroom of your students engaged in it. The "Sample Maker Manifesto" sidebar offers an example of what such a document might look like, and in the next section, you will find strategies you can use with a variety of stakeholders to develop your own. These strategies can be used anywhere from the classroom to the school system level.

As you create your Maker Manifesto, keep in mind the tenants of UDL and design thinking in order to be inclusive of all learners. Ideally, you should involve district and school leaders, maker champions, and even groups of parents and students—if developmentally and age appropriate—in the process of drafting your manifesto.

SAMPLE MAKER MANIFESTO

MAKER MANIFESTO

Making Is:

- An ongoing, continual process where students discover, design, and do work to deepen their understanding of the world.

- The ability to use that understanding to improve their own personal life as well as the lives of others, both locally and globally.

- A process that supports the development of personal dispositions that contribute to a culture that promotes empathy and awareness.

- Colliding different skill sets, intelligences, disciplines, and perspectives to create something new, relevant, and meaningful.

- A process that engages students in a safe environment (physically and emotionally) for strategic risk-taking and productive struggle.

- The ability to think flexibly from new perspectives to revise and refine ideas while at the same time embrace mistakes and unpredictable results.

- Taking individual ideas and amplifying them into something larger through a collaborative process.

- Supporting equitable access to tools, resources, spaces, and learning.

HOW-TO STRATEGIES:
Develop a Culture of Inclusive Maker Learning

The strategies in this section focus on collaborative brainstorming and idea evaluation to develop an inclusive definition of maker learning, comprise a Maker Champions cohort, as well as produce a Maker Manifesto to guide maker learning and makerspace development over time. (Remember to watch for the Signs and Signals icons aligned with each strategy, indicating which skills it supports for developing complex organizational change.)

STRATEGY 1.1: BRAIN WRITING AND TARGET STORMING

DURATION OF ACTIVITY: 30–45 minutes

RECOMMENDED NUMBER OF PEOPLE: 2 or more; 5 to 15 optimal

WHAT YOU'LL NEED:

- Sticky notes or index cards
- Sharpies or dry-erase markers
- Large poster paper or a large dry-erase board

The purpose of brain writing and target storming strategies is to work with a representative group of participants to identify key concepts that support the goals and purpose around maker learning and makerspaces. This is a necessary step before writing a definition of maker learning.

Although this activity can be done with a minimum of two participants, involving more stakeholders yields more diverse results. Some examples of diverse stakeholder perspectives include educators who work with different grade levels, student needs, and subject matter; families; students ranging from a variety of grade levels; district and building administrators; learning coaches; and librarians.

WHEN TO USE

The Brain Writing and Target Storming strategy is best to use when you are just getting started with identifying your core values around maker learning and the value it

HOW-TO STRATEGIES: DEVELOP A CULTURE OF INCLUSIVE MAKER LEARNING 29

> ### GO REMOTE
>
> - Use Padlet for generating categories for organizing identified themes. Padlet offers the opportunity to have participants sort the posts from the individual and collective brainstorm sessions into the appropriate categories. This can be done in real time or asynchronously.
> - One of the most powerful aspects of this activity is that it provides a process for generating and evaluating ideas, enabling participants to see individual ideas and move them around. To simulate that in a remote or virtual environment, use Google Slides to generate ideas, and then organize themes by moving slides around. Another way to mirror the face-to-face process remotely is to write ideas on paper Post-it Notes, and then use the Post-it App to snap photos of them, organize the photos, and share them. Similarly, you can use Google Jamboard to create and manipulate digital sticky notes.
> - To increase accessibility and personalization during this strategy, use Numbers or Pages to create multimodal notecards that can be accessed simultaneously by multiple users. Participants can contribute their ideas not only in text but also using audio clips.

brings to students. It also is a powerful activity that you can use any time you need to generate and evaluate ideas with others.

WHAT TO DO

STEP 1: Brainstorm individually. Ask people to work individually and silently for 5 to 7 minutes coming up with concepts or terms that they believe are essential to maker learning and makerspaces. The goal here is quantity. Encourage participants to keep it simple, writing words or phrases—not sentences—on their index cards.

STEP 2: Brainstorm collectively. Have participants work in groups of three to five for 8 to 10 minutes to review all cards around the room, starting with their small group. Remind participants that they can collaboratively brainstorm and create any new cards to fill in gaps with

> ### ALIGNED ISTE STANDARDS FOR EDUCATORS
>
> - Facilitator, 6d
> - Collaborator, 4a

what they feel may be missing. Remind participants to consider the organization's larger mission and vision around teaching and learning when doing this.

STEP 3: Generate categories. Bring the whole group together, and ask participants to identify themes or larger categories that emerge from the individual and collective brainstorm. Write these themes or categories on a large piece of paper, on a dry-erase board, or using a digital tool.

STEP 4: Sort cards. Have participants sort the cards from the individual and collective brainstorm sessions into the appropriate categories. You may want to write the categories or large themes on larger pieces of paper or at the top of a dry-erase board, and then post all other ideas under that category or theme. For example, if Design Thinking is a category that emerges, any card that falls under the Design Thinking category would go under that theme.

STEP 5: Check the environment. Have participants spend 20 to 30 minutes doing some research on maker learning. The ISTE Innovative Designer playlist is a great place to start. During this process, encourage participants to think about whether they would like to add anything. If they find information that backs up their own ideas, suggest they collect it in a collaborative document or space to provide as evidence when they are making their case to others.

STRATEGY 1.2: REPEAT AND REFINE

DURATION OF ACTIVITY: 15–20 minutes

RECOMMENDED NUMBER OF PEOPLE: Small or large groups

WHAT YOU'LL NEED:

- Sharpies or dry-erase markers
- Large poster paper, large dry-erase board, or collaborative document
- Sticky notes

The purpose of this strategy is to assist members in clarifying or redefining the purpose and value of maker learning. It also can be used to clarify or define a problem you may be working on as it relates to creating an inclusive maker culture. Although this activity can be implemented with a small group of participants, having a larger, more diverse group of participants will increase opportunities for inclusion.

GO REMOTE

- One of the benefits of this strategy is to generate a high quantity of initial ideas. Encourage group members to use voice-to-text or other accessibility features as a way of capturing their thoughts. Talking ideas out versus focusing on typing offers opportunities to support learner variation. Google Docs and the Notes app provide these easy-to-use accessibility supports.

- Because this strategy uses repetition and revision as a tactic for refining ideas, it is beneficial to use tools that assist participants in organizing. Participants can use Google Slides to write general statements per slide, and then use the bullet points or other formats to add the new revisions or paraphrasing. Similarly, Padlet offers many features for organizing statements, phrases, and questions in different layouts. Specifically, using the Timeline or Shelf formats provides participants with options to organize their ideas in a format that facilitates the organization and visualization of the idea refinement process.

WHEN TO USE

A good follow-up to Strategy 1.1, this strategy is best to use when you have a rough draft or have started to construct sentences after the brain writing and target storming activities. The Repeat and Refine activity is also very useful for engaging in anticipatory problem-solving or working through possible barriers.

WHAT TO DO

STEP 1: Write general statements that represent your preliminary view of maker learning or that identify a problem or barrier to being able to successfully create an inclusive maker culture. For example, on the whiteboard or in your collaborative document, you might write *teachers don't know what maker learning is*.

STEP 2: Divide the statement into key words, phrases, or questions. For example, *What is maker learning?*

ALIGNED ISTE STANDARDS FOR EDUCATORS

- Leader, 2c
- Collaborator, 4a

STEP 3: Use the group's keywords, phrases, or questions to come up with new words that can help you bring more specificity to the problem you are defining or the ideal state of maker learning you want to achieve. For example, *opportunities for all students to ask questions, seek solutions, or build and represent their ideas using digital tools.*

STEP 4: Repeat this paraphrasing, rewording as many times as possible, until you develop various ways to define maker learning or overcome any barriers.

STRATEGY 1.3: TELL ME WHY

DURATION OF ACTIVITY: 40+ minutes

RECOMMENDED NUMBER OF PEOPLE: 2 or more

WHAT YOU'LL NEED:

- Sharpies or dry-erase markers
- Large poster paper, large dry-erase board, or collaborative document
- Sticky notes

 The purpose of this strategy is to develop your concept of maker learning as well as to develop the why or rationale for your definition of maker learning. The why statements you create in this strategy can be very useful for further developing your definition of making, as well as to identify key components that support the why of your work. Having a clear why will be a valuable piece to help building understanding and validity around your work.

WHEN TO USE

The Tell Me Why strategy is best to use when you have a rough draft or have started to outline key concepts of ideal maker learning experiences, resources, or spaces.

WHAT TO DO

STEP 1: Create a T-chart. On the right side of chart write down essential "wants," adjectives, ideas, or outcomes

ALIGNED ISTE STANDARDS FOR EDUCATORS

- Analyst, 7a

of having an inclusive maker culture, resources, or makerspace that you want to achieve (Figure 1.2).

WANTS/IDEAS/OUTCOMES	
All students feel welcome and inspired.	
All teachers find an entry into maker learning.	
Maker learning can be high- or low-tech.	
Students must make and test prototypes.	

Figure 1.2 Start a T-chart to list the things you want to achieve.

STEP 2: Draw a line to the right side of the chart. With each element, consider why this is important and write down the answers on the right side of the chart (Figure 1.3).

WANTS/IDEAS/OUTCOMES	WHY IT MATTERS
All students feel welcome and inspired.	If students aren't comfortable or confident in navigating the challenge or the resources, they will be reluctant to engage.
All teachers find an entry into maker learning.	All industries are impacted by the rapid acceleration of technology.
Maker learning can be high- or low-tech.	Rapid prototyping is used in a variety of industries and serves a purpose.
Students must make and test prototypes.	Data literacy and visualization is an important skill. Students can develop these skills by making and testing prototypes.

Figure 1.3 Next, add the reasons why the things you want to achieve are important. This will be powerful for helping other stakeholder groups gain meaningful insights to the work and make connections to their own learning environments.

GO REMOTE

- Be aware of participants' needs prior to a virtual meeting and think about issues participants may have with seeing, hearing content, or manipulating a mouse or trackpad. Choose tools and methods that minimize possible limitations.
- Leverage the whiteboard and accessibility features of your videoconferencing tool to provide diversity in the different modalities participants can leverage to engage and participate. For example, Google Meet and Zoom allow participants to enable captions, plus Zoom enables participants to scroll back and review captions they may have missed.
- Use Padlet to organize a digital T-chart (items in one column and the why in another). Padlet's Reply and Rate features provide opportunities for participants to comment on, rank, or rate items in the chart.

STRATEGY 1.4: BRAINSTORMING AND DOT VOTING

DURATION OF ACTIVITY: 30–45 minutes

RECOMMENDED NUMBER OF PEOPLE: 3 or more

WHAT YOU'LL NEED:

- Markers
- Large poster paper
- 10 dot stickers per participant

The purpose of dot voting is to encourage collaboration and collectively assess elements that are deemed most essential to creating a powerful Maker Manifesto. Dot voting is most powerful with large groups involved. Not only does more participation increase the option to include different perspectives in the decision-making process, but the activity is also powerful for creating a visual representation of what people are thinking.

WHEN TO USE

The Brainstorming and Dot Voting strategy is great to use with your Maker Teacher Champions to develop your Maker Manifesto.

GO REMOTE

- Have participants use Google Docs or other software that supports collaborative documents to share their ideas and group ideas. Next, create a new document with a two-column table, and ask participants to paste their ideas in one side of the chart. Finally, ask participants to cast their ten votes by inserting shapes in the second column. Voting this way will create a nice visual representation and can be performed asynchronously or synchronously.

- Try **dotstorming.com**, which offers a powerful way to engage participants in virtual dot voting online. Participants receive a link to the voting board, which can be password protected, if desired. In addition, the manager of the board can choose to disable the chat or commenting features, as well as moderate participant anonymity. Participants can use different colors and shapes for their votes, which is a nice option for considering perception variability. The board manager can also add images to the board to represent information in ways beyond text.

- Gather all the ideas ahead of time from brainstorming using either a Google Doc or Google Form. Next, create a new form and use the multiple-choice grid question type to engage people in allocating their votes. In the form's rows, paste all the statements, and in the columns make an entry for each number of possible votes (1 through 10) that participants can cast for each statement. Participants then choose their desired vote count for the various statements and submit their form.

WHAT TO DO

STEP 1: Have participants work in groups of three to five to brainstorm ways to complete the sentence prompts *"Maker Learning..."* or *"Making is... ."* Spend about 8 to 10 minutes on this step and have each group list their ideas on a separate sheet of poster paper. Encourage participants to revisit the previously shared definition of maker learning, consider what it would look like to engage in maker learning, and think about what would help to identify if a behavior or space exemplifies or supports maker learning.

STEP 2: Place all the lists on the wall, and provide participants with time to silently review all posters.

STEP 3: Provide each person with 10 stickers, and explain to participants that they will be using the stickers to vote on the statements that speak most to the vision of maker learning. They can use as many of their stickers as they like on any statement, voting multiple times for a particular idea, but they are limited to 10 votes total. Remind participants to remain silent during this activity. This is a time for people to contemplate, not converse.

> **ALIGNED ISTE STANDARDS FOR EDUCATORS**
>
> o Analyst, 7a, b

STEP 4: Count the votes, and use the most highly rated statements to draft a Maker Manifesto.

Next Steps

- Create a definition of maker learning that aligns to your school system's values.

- Enlist teacher leader champions to bring depth to the definition of maker learning, explore new concepts, and test ideas.

- Develop a Maker Manifesto.

- Create a shared understanding of what prototyping is and how it is used in a variety of industries.

- Provide opportunities for educators and stakeholders to understand how all current initiatives connect to support the vision of your students and work.

- Incorporate details into your definition of maker learning and your Maker Manifesto that increase inclusivity and flexibility, for example, virtual and physical environments, high- and low-tech capacities, elements of the design thinking process, and language inspired by the Innovative Designer and Computational Thinker standards of the ISTE Standards for Students.

- Scan the Chapter 1 Resources QR code to check out useful links, templates, and resources for this chapter.

Chapter 1 Resources

Reflection

After reading Chapter 1, take some time to consider how its ideas apply within your context using the questions below.

- What is your why for developing a culture of maker learning and design thinking?
- What problems could you solve by incorporating these development strategies in a virtual environment?
- Explore some of the links shared or available on the chapter's resources page. Was there a resource or example that resonated with you? Why?

Develop a Systems-Based Approach to Inclusive Maker Learning

By the end of this chapter, you will:

- Build on what you learned in Chapter 1 about building an inclusive definition of maker learning to engage others in the work

- Evaluate a variety of strategies that can be used to spark innovation, generate new ideas, and evaluate and prioritize key components of successful student maker learning experiences and resources

View from the Field: Embracing Diverse Perspectives

Limited time. Simultaneously occurring projects. Urgent matters. There are many reasons professional learning opportunities for adults might just scratch the surface, and fall short of deeper thinking, heightened engagement, and authentic problem-solving. Adult learners need to be provided with opportunities to engage in professional learning that offers opportunities for voice and choice in the way information is presented, new learning is constructed, and skills are demonstrated. The different positions educators hold within their school system also provide an opportunity to bring more diversity and perspectives into the culture you are developing. It is important to provide a variety of options for the different members within a school system to contribute to the development of an inclusive maker learning culture. This chapter provides a variety of opportunities to engage diverse stakeholder groups in this work.

Connecting the Dots and Building Capacity

Envisioning an ideal state of maker learning is a powerful way to identify and model the desired elements of maker learning within a school system. This type of envisioning and illustrating why maker learning matters can assist educators in identifying and developing the skills students need to grow as innovative designers and computational thinkers. It is also important for educators to begin identifying places in their current curriculum where these learning experiences can transpire. This chapter focuses on the importance of integrating your definition of maker learning into the larger goals of your school system.

One of the most powerful things that school leaders can do is to connect the dots between seemingly different initiatives that are taking place simultaneously. For example, if a school system is working on initial implementation or continuous improvement in the areas of:

- Universal Design for Learning
- Digital learning and 1:1 device access
- Maker learning and design thinking

One way to connect these initiatives is to communicate how each is a piece of the larger puzzle. Each individual piece is needed and serves a purpose for helping the other pieces fit together. Moreover, in order to deepen stakeholder understanding, it is important to visualize these connections among projects, goals, and initiatives when they are presented to various stakeholder groups. Tables 2.1–2.3 offer a step-by-step example of how to construct your school system's big-picture puzzle in a way that assists stakeholders in understanding how different elements of the work are connected and support one another.

TABLE 2.1 Step 1: Define the Puzzle Pieces

UNIVERSAL DESIGN FOR LEARNING	DIGITAL LEARNING AND 1:1 PROGRAMMING	MAKER LEARNING AND DESIGN THINKING
Provides the large perspective on how to reach different needs of students through intentional instructional design.	The ways students use digital and learning technologies to do and show learning to prepare for the current and future world.	The type of innovative thinker and learner we want to develop who demonstrates technological, data, and human literacies.

TABLE 2.2 Step 2: Show How the Puzzle Pieces Can Fit Together

TEACHER PLANNING UNIVERSAL DESIGN FOR LEARNING	PROCESS AND TOOLS DIGITAL LEARNING AND 1:1 PROGRAMMING	TYPE OF LEARNER MAKERS: COMPUTATIONAL THINKERS AND INNOVATIVE DESIGNERS
UDL is a framework to improve and optimize teaching and learning for all people based on scientific insights into how humans learn. UDL principles outline elements educators can use to construct inclusive learning experiences. • Representation • Engagement • Action and Expression	The way we do and show learning. We use digital tools and practices to engage in collaboration, critical thinking, creativity, and communication. This allows us to: • Provide mechanisms for how teachers represent information • Support workflow • Provide students with tools they can use to engage in learning and express their learning outcomes in personalized ways	The type of innovative thinker and learner we want to develop to be prepared for college, career, and life in a rapidly, technologically advancing world. Students are inventive problem-solvers, using a design thinking process, making and creating solutions with unique tools and capacities. They can demonstrate learning with voice and choice through the development of authentic solutions, making and testing of prototypes.

CONNECTING THE DOTS AND BUILDING CAPACITY 41

STOP & JOT: List the current initiatives, goals, or projects your school system is working on. Choose which ones most relate to the work of building an inclusive maker culture, then brainstorm possible connections between these areas of focus and inclusive maker learning.

TABLE 2.3 Step 3: Demonstrate How Teachers Can Strategically Use the Puzzle Pieces Daily to Support Learning

TEACHER ACTION	CORRESPONDING INITIATIVE
Identify an empathy-driven problem or challenge for students to solve. Incorporate skills outlined by the Innovative Designer and Computational Thinker ISTE Standards for Students.	• Maker Learning • Universal Design for Learning: *Representation and Engagement*
Allow for student choice in a solution of how they would solve a problem, providing student voice and choice in how they create their prototype solution.	• Maker Learning • Universal Design for Learning: *Representation, Engagement, Action, and Expression*
Use digital learning practices to engage in the 4Cs (critical thinking, collaboration, creativity, and communications) through the design process. Digital learning practices and 1:1 technology access support how students are communicating, collaborating, and thinking about/planning their creative solutions.	• Maker Learning • Universal Design for Learning: *Representation and Engagement* • Digital Learning and 1:1 Technology Access
Provide unique tools and capacities to create prototypes of solutions to test, iterate, gather feedback, and modify.	• Maker Learning • Universal Design for Learning: *Representation, Engagement, Action, and Expression* • Digital Learning and 1:1 Technology Access

HOW-TO STRATEGIES:
Creating Breakthroughs

Extending your work from Chapter 1, the focus of the ready-to-use strategies in this chapter is to guide education professionals in big-picture goal setting and visioning for aligning and embedding maker learning into your larger goals of curriculum, instruction, and assessment. You'll also find strategies to help you identify, evaluate, and prioritize what next steps and resources will be needed. As you're sorting through which strategies to try, remember that your team needs to be able to connect the dots of maker learning within the larger context of their current work to avoid organizational fatigue.

STRATEGY 2.1: UNPACKING THE BOXES

DURATION OF ACTIVITY: 25+ minutes

RECOMMENDED NUMBER OF PEOPLE: 4 or more

WHAT YOU'LL NEED:

○ Space to share your ideas that all participants can access

The purpose of this strategy is to assist a diverse group of participants in identifying possible barriers that create limitations on an inclusive maker learning environment. You could also use this strategy to generate possible solutions for overcoming specific barriers that have been previously identified. Either way, the outcome of this activity is to help stakeholders visualize the ideal categories or characteristics of an inclusive maker learning culture.

WHEN TO USE

The Unpacking the Boxes strategy works well after you have a developed a definition of maker learning and a Maker Manifesto. It is a powerful strategy for helping stakeholders break down concepts of maker learning and gain insight into which concepts are most direct. Because the nature of this activity is to identify or problem solve around barriers to successful maker learning and inclusion, it is very important to incorporate participants who can share different experiences and perspectives. Choose a platform or materials that allow for flexibility and multiple people to contribute.

WHAT TO DO

STEP 1: Create a square or box to represent your center. Inside this box, write down a specific element of your maker learning definition that you want to explore or a possible problem you think you may encounter, such as *Maker learning isn't for all subject areas*.

STEP 2: Draw a second box around the first box and write down the most direct and immediate concepts that describe or relate to what you wrote inside the first box. For example, you could add a question like *Why does this problem exist?* or an issue like *Teachers aren't familiar with the design thinking process*.

STEP 3: Repeat Step 2 around the second box, adding more boxes and statements to your drawing (Figure 2.1). If you are identifying core values, the concepts farthest away from the core will reveal boundaries. If you are identifying core problems, the outer boxes will help you

> **ALIGNED ISTE STANDARDS FOR EDUCATORS LEADER**
>
> ○ Learner, 1c
> ○ Leader, 2c

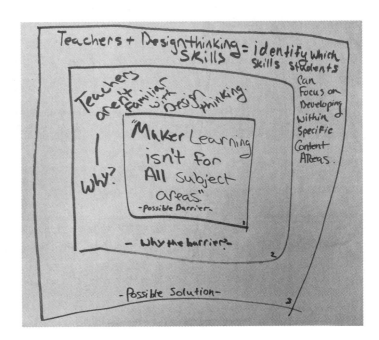

Figure 2.1 Use the concentric squares to identify and organize possible barriers that create limitations on an inclusive maker learning environment, as well as brainstorm possible solutions.

> **GO REMOTE**
>
> - Google Jamboard is a collaborative whiteboard app that allows participants to collaboratively draw in a virtual space. Provide each group with a specific board on Google Jamboard to keep their work organized and separate.
> - Google Draw allows participants to meet in a virtual space to create graphics and label them. Participants can also move text boxes around within the shapes they create. Provide a ready-made box template as a Google Doc or Google Draw file to participants to save time and assist them in more easily visualizing the steps of the task.
> - PollUnit (**pollunit.com**) is an online tool that provides a variety of ways for participants to brainstorm, share, and vote on ideas. Participants can also share photos and images, which can be powerful for visualizing literal barriers in the space as well as possible solutions.

work toward identifying possible things to address to get to a solution. A sample conclusion might be *We need to help teachers become more familiar with the design thinking process and identify which specific skills students can focus on developing within specific content areas.* This strategy is important for narrowing your core values for inclusive maker learning and prioritizing. It also can be a powerful way to identify possible solutions or areas in your work that need more attention.

STRATEGY 2.2: ON THE COVER

DURATION OF ACTIVITY: 45–90 minutes

RECOMMENDED NUMBER OF PEOPLE: 2 or more

WHAT YOU'LL NEED:

- The On the Cover template (downloadable from Chapter 2 Resources)
- Markers, pencils, colored pencils, or a tool that allows you to annotate on a PDF or image file
- Space to share your ideas that all participants can access

The purpose of this activity is to engage participants in envisioning an ideal, future state of specific components of maker learning. This open-ended and highly visual activity allows for creative thinking.

WHEN TO USE

Very effective for helping participants visualize what success would look like, the On the Cover activity works best when you are ready to expand on an existing definition of maker learning and Maker Manifesto. It can be hard for people to envision something that doesn't exist yet, which is why engaging participants in this type of anticipatory visioning work is important.

WHAT TO DO

STEP 1: *Generate focus topics.* Assign participants into groups of three to four. Before gathering participants, create a list or cards of sample maker learning themes or resources. You can find sample cards to help you get started in the digital resources for this chapter.

STEP 2: *Dive into an area of focus.* Explain to participants that they will create a magazine cover story about what they envision for an ideal state of maker learning. Using your list of sample maker learning themes or resources, assign participant groups a specific topic to focus on. When assigning multiple topics and concepts, remind participants that the concepts can be combined or explored separately. In addition, be sure to:

- Encourage participants to consider what successes with maker learning would look like in an ideal state.

- Encourage participants to draw from experience, imagine what they think it ideally could look like, or a little bit of both. If groups initially aren't sure about their topic or don't have firsthand experience, encourage them to conduct some brief research to see what others have learned about maker learning.

- Remind participants to write their cover story in past tense and with enthusiasm to help convey what an ideal state could look like.

STEP 3: *Brainstorm what ideal looks like.* The biggest thing you can do to be successful with this activity is to provide participants with the time to discuss, brainstorm, and

GO REMOTE

- The Notes app (for iPad or iPhone) and Kami offer great ways to annotate PDFs and images, making it easy for participants to mark up the pre-created template. These tools also provide opportunities to easily share content with others. The ability to share cover stories across groups creates opportunities to extend the conversation and to allow participants to better understand perspectives of other groups and variables that shape inclusive maker learning.
- If you are looking to give participants directions but also the freedom to design their own template or an on-the-cover or webpage look, Canva is a graphic design tool that is easy to use and offers collaborative features.
- Collaborative creation tools such as Pages, Keynote, and Adobe Spark provide highly visual opportunities for participants to design their own cover while also offering multiple file export options. It is also important that groups can export their cover story and post to a shared place for others to see. To conduct a virtual gallery walk of sorts, use Padlet, Google Sites, or features of your learning management system that allow participants to share and view the work of others.

visualize what their ideal state looks like (Figure 2.2). Remind participants to imagine the best-case scenario for inclusive maker learning and take it one step further in their scenarios. Encourage participants to first spend five quiet minutes imagining their own story, and then to work with others to generate the "story of the year."

While participants are brainstorming, set a timer or provide a link to a specific music timer video on YouTube that participants can access whether they are in breakout rooms or in a whole group video conference.

STEP 4: *Create a cover story.* Remind participants of the elements of a good cover story, and encourage them to:

- Brainstorm to document initial ideas for the cover story. What are the big ideas?
- Tell the *big* story of success. This will be featured on a magazine cover. What visuals would capture the major themes?

ALIGNED ISTE STANDARDS FOR EDUCATORS

- Collaborator, 4a
- Analyst, 7a

- Craft a headline to convey the substance of the cover story. What single statement would catch someone's interest?

- Add sidebars to reveal interesting facets of the cover story. What would be interesting topics for a deeper dive?

- Include quotes from anyone related to the story. What would teachers, students, families, community, or administrators say if this were successful?

- Support the content with illustrations. What photos would help people better understand the story, its important takeaways, or the concepts it describes?

STEP 5: *Share.* Have groups share their stories with each other and discuss the creations!

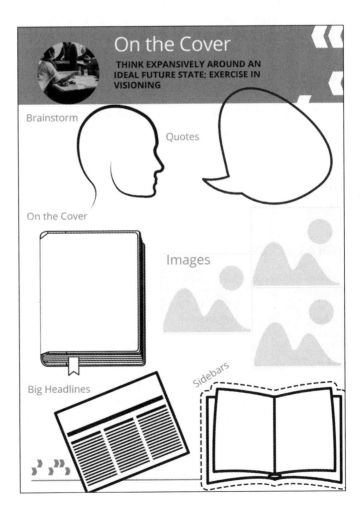

Figure 2.2 While participants discuss, brainstorm, and visualize what their ideal state looks like, supply a template to assist them in visualizing next steps.

STRATEGY 2.3: PLANNING A DISASTER

DURATION OF ACTIVITY: 20–60 minutes

RECOMMENDED NUMBER OF PEOPLE: Multiple groups of 2–4

WHAT YOU'LL NEED:

- Space to curate ideas so that all participants can access

The purpose of this strategy is to assist participants in diving deeper into an existing or anticipated problem or barrier that might be faced when developing an inclusive maker culture. This strategy is also great for working toward new solutions or ideas that may not typically come up in a traditional solution-generating session.

WHEN TO USE

When different points of view surface or when a group needs to engage in anticipatory problem solving, this strategy can help. While you can use Planning a Disaster with a small number of participants, it's most effective when you have as many participants and different viewpoints as possible. At the same time, when dividing participants into groups, remember that the smaller the group the more likely it will be to have open dialogue.

WHAT TO DO

STEP 1: *Create a four-column chart.* In the first column, write down a list of events describing either barriers to inclusive maker learning or a related problem you want to solve. An example barrier could be *students aren't provided with the opportunities to develop their own authentic solutions.*

STEP 2: *Plan the disaster.* In the second column, expand on the events you have put together in the first column by thinking of what it would look like if it were a worst-case scenario. An example worst-case scenario might be *teachers always tell students what they are making.*

ALIGNED ISTE STANDARDS FOR EDUCATORS

- Designer, 5b
- Facilitator, 6a

Students aren't diving into the problem they are solving and don't know who they are making for.

STEP 3: *Avert the worst-case scenario.* Think of ways to prevent this worst-case scenario, and write them in the third column. What would need to be in place to prevent the items in column two from happening? For example, you could provide teachers with guidance and time to differentiate between teacher-directed and student-directed making, or you could develop scenarios that represent both examples and non-examples of student-centered, authentic problem-solving and have teachers categorize and analyze the scenarios. Focus on the questions:

- What am I making?
- Who am I making for?
- Why am I making?

STEP 4: *Brainstorm preventative ideas or strategies.* In column four, construct a list of preventative ideas or strategies that you could use to develop next steps to overcome or avoid the initial problem or barrier identified. Then provide time for people to discuss items in column four and finalize next steps or action items.

> ### GO REMOTE
>
> - To help participants focus on the task at hand, it is beneficial to provide participants with a template that they can use to share their ideas and group ideas. Specifically, Google Docs makes it easy to provide participants with a template from which they can make a "forced copy" to save time. To do so, after the last forward-slash of the document's URL, replace the word *edit* with *copy*. Now when you share this modified URL with others, it will automatically prompt users to "make their own copy" of the document.
>
> - It can be hard for participants to brainstorm possible barriers or to visualize what a less-than-ideal scenario might look like. Videoconferencing tools and breakout rooms are highly recommended to enhance real-time conversations during the small group work of this strategy. Moderators of the activity should take time to visit the breakout rooms of different groups to see if they have any questions and to check in on progress. Also, videoconferencing whiteboard features provide participants with a way to visualize their thinking.

CHAPTER 2: DEVELOP A SYSTEMS-BASED APPROACH TO INCLUSIVE MAKER LEARNING

STRATEGY 2.4: BOTH SIDES OF THE STORY

DURATION OF ACTIVITY: 35–45 minutes

RECOMMENDED NUMBER OF PEOPLE: 3 or more

WHAT YOU'LL NEED:

- Space to write or type your ideas so that all participants can see and contribute

The purpose of this strategy is to assist members in developing new patterns of thinking, by developing a story that brings clarity to the stakeholders directly or indirectly involved in contributing to your maker culture.

ALIGNED ISTE STANDARDS FOR EDUCATORS

- Collaborator, 4a, 4b

WHEN TO USE

The Both Sides of the Story strategy works well when you are working to identify the various roles stakeholders can play or if you have stakeholders in your system that have different perspectives on maker learning and how to make it successful.

WHAT TO DO

STEP 1: Create a chart with two columns; you can do this as a whole group. In the first column, describe a specific current state as it relates to maker learning in your school system. Keep your response short, either one paragraph or sentence, such as *Teachers are not sure how to engage students in process-driven maker work in a virtual environment.*

STEP 2: In the second column, list all the stakeholders or variables you think are directly or indirectly a part of the scenario you described in the first column. For example, you could write *Teachers, Students, Technology.*

STEP 3: Break the whole group into smaller groups, and have each group make a copy of the original T-chart.

STEP 4: To gather stakeholder perspectives, have each group member focus on the perspective of an individual stakeholder listed in column two. In other words, person one takes the perspective of the teacher, person two takes the students, and person three takes technology.

STEP 5: Explain to the groups that they'll now begin to focus on telling a story from the unique perspectives of their stakeholders or variables. Have them each create a new chart of three columns and several rows, as shown in Figure 2.3. For groups larger than two, start with two of the identified stakeholders or variables and have the third group member be the observer and note taker.

GO REMOTE

- When engaging participants in this activity in a remote environment, use videoconferencing tools and breakout rooms to enhance real-time conversations. Before the meeting starts, set up breakout rooms with time constraints to keep participants on track and streamline the time spent during the meeting.

- Although it might be tempting to just collect artifacts from the groups, it is more important to ask all teams to rejoin the whole group videoconference to share out their final highlights. Having participants use screensharing features allows them to take control of their share-out and have more responsibility.

- In addition to holding a whole group share-out, it also can be productive to provide participants a shared space to post final statements that capture the values and perspectives of the different stakeholders and variables.

PROBLEM/CURRENT STATE: **TEACHERS AREN'T SURE HOW TO ENGAGE STUDENTS IN PROCESS-DRIVEN MAKER WORK IN A VIRTUAL ENVIRONMENT.**		
Words	Stakeholder/Variable 1: Teacher	Stakeholder/Variable 2: Technology
Word 1		
Word 2		
Word 3		
Word 4		
Word 5		
Word 6		

Figure 2.3 Have participants create a chart to organize information about the various roles that stakeholders can play or the different perspectives stakeholders have on maker learning and how to make it successful.

STEP 6: Have the two participants who represent the stakeholder/variable take turns saying one word per turn that represents their point of view, values, or a position they hold at the time. Continue this process until the group thinks that specific sentences or statements can be formed (Figure 2.4).

PROBLEM/CURRENT STATE: **TEACHERS AREN'T SURE HOW TO ENGAGE STUDENTS IN PROCESS-DRIVEN MAKER WORK IN A VIRTUAL ENVIRONMENT.**		
Words	Stakeholder/Variable 1: Teacher	Stakeholder/Variable 2: Technology
Word 1	Ongoing work	Live
Word 2	Steps to complete	Collaborative
Word 3	Reflection	Multimedia
Word 4	Artifacts	Drafts
Word 5	Timelines, deadlines	Reflective
Word 6	Self-directed	Personalized

Figure 2.4 Participants brainstorm and add key terms that relate to stakeholder points of view, values, or positions they hold.

STEP 7: Once key terms are identified for each side, the team should work together to write out statements that capture the values and perspectives of the different stakeholders and variables, as shown in Figure 2.5.

HOW-TO STRATEGIES: CREATING BREAKTHROUGHS 53

PROBLEM/CURRENT STATE: *TEACHERS AREN'T SURE HOW TO ENGAGE STUDENTS IN PROCESS-DRIVEN MAKER WORK IN A VIRTUAL ENVIRONMENT.*		
Variables	Stakeholder/Variable 1: Teacher	Stakeholder/Variable 2: Technology
Statements	Teachers can develop a timeline of steps students can complete during the ongoing steps of a project.	Google Sites allows students to curate artifacts using multimedia tools to document outcomes of learning.

Figure 2.5 Use the key terms to write statements that represent the stakeholders' values and perspectives.

STEP 8: After developing key statements that represent multiple perspectives, highlight and identify the words or phrases that could lead to new ideas or solutions. Elaborate on the new ideas based on analyzing the two lines of thinking. This process will allow you to form new statements that consider multiple stakeholder perspectives or variables. Based on Figure 2.4, for example, a group might come up with *Maker learning can take place in a virtual learning environment. Teachers can outline key timelines, artifacts, and requirements for how students can capture and reflect on the stages of their design process. Digital and physical resources allow students to make and test prototypes.*

STRATEGY 2.5: WHERE TO?

DURATION OF ACTIVITY: 60–90 minutes

RECOMMENDED NUMBER OF PEOPLE: 3 or more

WHAT YOU'LL NEED:

- Space to write or type ideas that all participants can see

The purpose of this strategy is to engage participants in exploring potential problems that would prevent an inclusive maker culture from thriving.

ALIGNED ISTE STANDARDS FOR EDUCATORS

- Collaborator, 4a, 4b

> ### GO REMOTE
>
> - When using collaborative documents from Google Docs, Pages, or elsewhere, assign specific groups or participants to designated tables to share their responses. Likewise, using Padlet, the Shelf, or Canvas format can be very useful for doing this activity in an online environment.
> - Videoconferencing tools are highly recommended to enhance real-time conversations during these activities. Specifically, maximizing breakout rooms can assist in this process. Zoom and some other platforms now allow you to create breakout rooms ahead of time, and if participants know the name of their group, they can select and join that specific room. This will save time compared to assigning participants to separate breakout rooms prior to the activity.
> - Ask all teams to share out their final highlights, encouraging them to use screensharing to present any visuals they have. If the highlights are in a shared document that the moderator has access to, the moderator can present the content while the group members talk.

WHEN TO USE

The Where To? strategy is best to use when stakeholders are at the stage of identifying possible barriers to the success of inclusive maker learning. It is valuable to anticipate, identify, and confront possible barriers before they emerge.

WHAT TO DO

STEP 1: List current barriers, issues, or problems participants see or anticipate encountering in their work to develop an inclusive maker learning culture. Then draw a line extending to the right from each statement, such as *Prototyping is not clearly understood across content areas—*

STEP 2: To the right of the line, list a solution idea. Remind participants to use as much detail as possible, for example: *Prototyping is not clearly understood across content areas—Students can use a variety of mediums to visualize their ideas and solutions.*

STEP 3: Outline how to avoid the obstacle, for example:

- Identify and evaluate different ways prototyping is used within various industries.
- Align these industries to content area standards or work.
- Outline and help stakeholders visualize high- and low-tech opportunities for prototyping.

STRATEGY 2.6: MAKERSPACE RESOURCE PRIORITIZATION

DURATION OF ACTIVITY: 10–20 minutes

RECOMMENDED NUMBER OF PEOPLE: 2 or more

WHAT YOU'LL NEED:

- 10 dot stickers per person
- Worksheet that lists categories and sample visuals of items that fit the category

The purpose of this activity is to collaboratively identify and prioritize resources for outfitting a shared makerspace. It is very similar to Strategy 1.4, Brainstorming & Dot Voting. Providing key, pre-identified categories is helpful for prioritizing purchasing needs. Remember to focus on categories of resources, not specific items.

WHEN TO USE

There are many lists and recommendations of specific tools, technologies, and capacities for makerspaces and maker learning. These details and budgeting can also be overwhelming when first starting out. The Makerspace Resource Prioritization activity helps participants take a step back and consider the larger categories that your space and students will need, prior to diving into the details. Beyond identifying categories of needs, it can help you align budgets to needs prior to procuring resources.

> **ALIGNED ISTE STANDARDS FOR EDUCATORS**
> - Facilitator, 6b, 6c
> - Analyst, 7a

GO REMOTE

- Use Google Docs to have participants share their ideas via collaborative documents. Create a new document with a two-column table, and ask participants to paste in their responses into the left column. Finally, ask participants to cast their ten votes by inserting shapes in the second column. Because people aren't supposed to talk during this activity, it can be performed asynchronously or synchronously.
- If you gather all the ideas ahead of time from brainstorming, you can use Google Forms to create a multiple-choice-question grid to engage people in allocating their votes. In the rows, paste all the statements, and in the columns make an entry for each number of possible votes (1 through 10) that participants can cast for each statement.
- Padlet's Shelf format can be used to organize categories and incorporate visual examples into each. Allow participants to type how many of their votes they want to use for that specific category.

WHAT TO DO

STEP 1: Post various categories of makerspace resources and visual examples of what might fit into the categories in a place where all participants can view. Provide each participant with ten dot stickers.

STEP 2: Have participants circulate around silently, allocating their dots into categories they want to prioritize. Remind participants to think about categories, not individual samples of tools or resources.

STEP 3: Sum the votes for each category, and rank perceived needs.

HOW-TO STRATEGIES: CREATING BREAKTHROUGHS   57

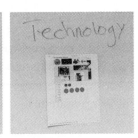

Figure 2.6 Dot voting provides a powerful way for stakeholders to weigh in on which categories of resources are most needed. This can lead to deeper conversations later about specific resources that need to be procured.

STRATEGY 2.7: TRUE FOR WHO

DURATION OF ACTIVITY: 45–60 minutes

RECOMMENDED NUMBER OF PEOPLE: 5 or more

WHAT YOU'LL NEED:

○ Space to share your ideas so all can see

The purpose of this strategy is to assist members in identifying and prioritizing resources for inclusive maker learning based on needs. This strategy is also useful if people on your team have different perspectives about the types of resources to invest in. This activity can also be used to focus on identifying and building out key beliefs about maker learning if you aren't ready to focus on resources.

ALIGNED ISTE STANDARDS FOR EDUCATORS

○ Collaborator, 4b

WHEN TO USE

The True for Who strategy is best to use when you are working to identify resources to support maker learning. This activity can be especially helpful for when you hit a roadblock, if elements that you didn't anticipate surface, or if stakeholders hold differing opinions.

WHAT TO DO

STEP 1: Make two columns, and name them "Facts" About Maker Learning and "Opposites."

STEP 2: Use the "Facts" column to write down all the things that you hear people say or that they think are true about maker learning or resources (Figure 2.7).

"FACTS" ABOUT MAKER LEARNING	"OPPOSITES"
Maker learning can take place in any classroom.	
Students need consumable materials for prototyping.	
Extra storage isn't necessary.	
Maker learning can't take place in a remote environment.	

Figure 2.7 Participants start by writing down statements they've heard about maker learning.

STEP 3: In the second column, write down the opposite of every fact listed. This is where participants can get creative (Figure 2.8).

> ### GO REMOTE
>
> - To streamline the process, gather all the ideas and perceived facts ahead of time from brainstorming (using either Google Docs or Google Forms). Create a new form with Google Forms, and have participants indicate whether they feel the statements are true or not true. Then after each question, ask people to share their reasoning.
> - Using apps like Pear Deck and Nearpod also can allow people to vote and share their thinking. These tools can be used either synchronously or asynchronously for participant voting. Because they work with slide decks or presentation tools, place each of the statements on a slide and provide an opportunity for participants to vote or indicate the level to which they believe the statement is true for them.

"FACTS" ABOUT MAKER LEARNING	"OPPOSITES"
Maker learning can take place in any classroom.	A space dedicated to maker resources allows for more flexibility.
Students need consumable materials for prototyping.	There are many technologies and digital tools that can support different types of prototype creation.
Extra storage isn't necessary.	Students need a place to keep ongoing work.
Maker learning can't take place in a remote environment.	Students can use online portfolio tools to document stages of the design thinking process while they do maker learning in a remote environment.

Figure 2.8 Use the second column to write down the opposite of every statement listed. Then use these opposites to evaluate whether the "facts" still hold up.

STEP 4: Create a new list that has both "facts" and opposites in one column, then two more columns labeled "Not True" and "True," respectively. Ask a group of your maker champion teachers, administrators, or other relevant parties involved in your maker work to identify what is true for them according to their experiences. This also is a powerful place to engage students in the work.

STEP 5: Have participants write down or record their reasoning behind their choice, asking, "Why do you think _____ is true?" After analyzing the perceived facts and reasons why, it will be easier to categorize where people's thinking is at and identify next steps for your work.

STRATEGY 2.8: STUDENT STANDARDS IN ACTION: SCAVENGER HUNT

DURATION OF ACTIVITY: 45–75 minutes

RECOMMENDED NUMBER OF PEOPLE: Small groups, 2–4 participants per group

WHAT YOU'LL NEED:

- A digital space where educators can upload images or other digital content that they create

The purpose of this strategy is to help educators identify examples of current student work that demonstrates the skills of design thinking in action.

ALIGNED ISTE STANDARDS FOR EDUCATORS

- Analyst, 7b, 7c

WHEN TO USE

The Student Standards in Action: Scavenger Hunt strategy is very useful for helping educators think more deeply about the skills of design thinking and the ISTE Standards for Students and for Educators in general by looking for things they are already doing. This strategy is highly valuable if you anticipate that educators may view the integration of design thinking, maker learning skills, or the ISTE Standards for Students as "one more thing." It is important to remember that the ISTE Standards are aspirational. In other words, you don't have to meet all of them

> ## GO REMOTE
>
> - Encourage participants to use Google Slides, Microsoft PowerPoint, or Keynote to collaboratively work on a shared slide deck. You could also provide each group with a slide designated for their work and the skills or standards they are focusing on. These collaborative documents will be very useful for sharing out.
> - Remind participants that taking screenshots of student work that exists in a digital format is an option too.
> - Flipgrid allows participants to create a video and post it to an online topic, sharing it with others who have access to the topic. Encouraging participants to create a short video that reviews their findings can provide an additional opportunity for them to share and view the findings of others. Furthermore, because Flipgrid is video-based, it also provides a way to curate and revisit the outcomes of this activity at a later date or potentially share them with another audience.

to be successful. Instead, consider them a framework to prepare students with the necessary skills for tomorrow. It also is important to celebrate high-impact examples or pockets of where this work may already exist.

This strategy works especially well if educators can work in collaborative groups with grade-level or content-area colleagues. Taking this collaborative approach allows participants the opportunity to engage in powerful conversations and evaluate the current work of their students through the context of the standards.

WHAT TO DO

STEP 1: Identify which specific standard and skills you would like teachers to focus on.

STEP 2: Assign these standards and skills to specific groups of educators. Have participants discuss what specific skills are represented within the standards they are assigned.

STEP 3: Have educators go on a scavenger hunt during which they look in their classrooms or online learning spaces and gather examples of student work or curriculum that engage students in the skills and standards. Participants can take photos, video, or screenshots to capture what they find.

STEP 4: Have participants put at least three photos and the corresponding standard on a shared slide deck workspace that all participants have access to (Figure 2.9).

STEP 5: Gather all participants together for a collective share-out.

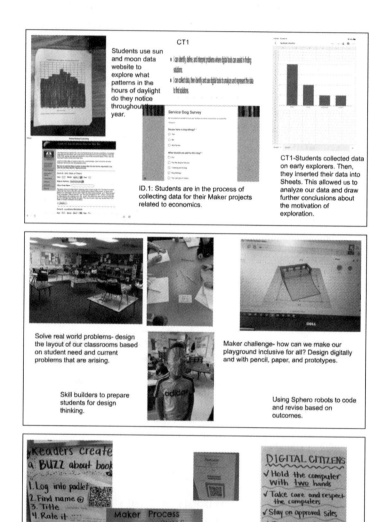

Figure 2.9 Encourage educators to identify and visualize examples of current student work that demonstrates the ISTE Standards in action.

Next Steps

- Create a schedule for when and how you will engage champions and other stakeholders when appropriate for next step skill development.
- Select strategies and activities that will assist stakeholders in developing foundational knowledge and understanding of inclusive maker learning.
- Align the current definition and vision of inclusive maker learning with other current school system initiatives, goals, or projects.
- Identify possible barriers to success and engage in anticipatory problem-solving.
- Provide opportunities for additional administrators and school leaders to gain deeper insight into and engage in sense-making activities about the vision of inclusive maker learning.
- Identify classifications of resources for champions and select stakeholders to consider as they participate in maker resource evaluation and procurement.
- Scan the Chapter 2 Resources QR code to check out useful links, templates, and resources for this chapter.

Chapter 2 Resources

Reflection

After reading Chapter 2, take some time to consider how its ideas apply within your context using the questions below.

- Why would it be advantageous to identify possible barriers you may face in your efforts to create a shared vision around inclusive maker learning?
- Consider different stakeholder groups in your school system. What methods or strategies would be most productive for confronting possible misunderstandings or presumptions?
- How might your process for planning, evaluating, and procuring resources positively contribute to your overall inclusive vision of maker learning?

Integrate UDL Guidelines Into Maker Experiences

By the end of this chapter, you will:

- Evaluate methods for integrating the Universal Design for Learning Guidelines within the maker learning process, resources, or makerspaces

- Gain specific instructional resources and strategies that support the development of expert learners

- Have the tools necessary to adapt and implement the resources provided into a variety of learning environments

- Understand how a makerspace can be either physical, virtual, or both

View from the Field: Do We Need a Space for Making?

Creating an inclusive vision around maker learning and connecting the dots between design thinking, maker learning, standards, and curriculum are crucial steps in the process of deciding who needs access to resources to support maker learning. Maker experiences should offer all teachers and students the opportunity to develop skill sets and dispositions that are a necessity for a rapidly technologically advancing world.

One thing that may not be clear, however, is whether a specific space dedicated to providing the resources to support maker learning is necessary. The recent increase in virtual- and remote-learning environments makes this question even more challenging. Some people believe that having maker resources on a cart that teachers check out and bring to their classrooms can be sufficient. Others believe having an agile space dedicated to design and making is valuable. Still others say that maker learning can take place anywhere, so specific spaces for this work are unnecessary. So, what's the right answer? I believe we should be asking a different question, instead, and that educators should focus more on the accessibility and inclusivity of the learning experience, resources, and spaces being explored. If you are considering creating a makerspace or design studio, ask yourself "What does a makerspace offer to our learners that a traditional classroom does not?"

Maker learning is more than engaging students in rapid prototyping; it's about offering resources: physical, technological, and spatial. Many schools find that most traditional classrooms aren't equipped to offer such options. Specifically, considering space for students to move about to test prototypes, store works in progress, and have access to a variety of technologies to support technological literacy development can be a key factor. This is also an important element when it comes to creating inclusive and accessible maker learning experiences. Specific attention must be brought to the accessibility of spaces and resources for making. Exploring these questions enables educators to focus on what resources would best empower all students to maximize student engagement in the design process.

Creating Inclusive Spaces for Maker Learning

No matter what your resources for making look like, first focus on developing a student maker mindset and skills. If you do so, students are more likely to intentionally use the resources they have. For students to be successful in this process, it is crucial for educators to be able to identify specific skill sets they desire students to develop. As discussed in Chapter 1, the ISTE Standards for Students, especially the Innovative Designer and Computational Thinker standards, provide an excellent lens through which to evaluate the skills and mindset students need, as well as the types of experiences and resources to provide to help them.

When it comes to key elements that truly differentiate maker learning from other inquiry-based learning practices, maker learning and design thinking require the building and testing of prototypes. The process of prototyping also demands the need for tools, technologies, capacities, and agile learning spaces that typical classrooms do not have the capacity or funding for. Furthermore, when matched with a diverse set of capacities, makerspaces not only provide access to a wide array of rapid prototyping materials, tools, and technologies but also tend to provide more agile learning spaces than traditional classrooms.

In addition, shared makerspaces can provide an opportunity to facilitate best instructional practices. This chapter demonstrates how you can outfit a makerspace to model and facilitate high-impact instructional and learning practices.

High-impact makerspaces provide:

- Storage solutions that hold a wide variety of tools, technologies, and capacities for making and building prototypes and are organized to be accessible to all learners

- Room and resources for making thinking visible, physically moving ideas around, and working in collaborative and co-working settings

- Agile spaces for sketching, building, storing, and showcasing prototypes

- Ability for learners to use the physical space in ways that support learning by doing while they plan, create, and test prototypes

To increase accessibility of maker learning for all students, tools and capacities should be digital as well as physical or mechanical, because digital tools allow learners to capitalize on many accessibility features. To that end, the strategies and resources presented in this chapter, and its companion Chapter 4, are intended to work in a variety of learning environments and are also highly effective for developing inclusive maker learning experiences in remote or virtual learning environments. Test out and explore new methods for student skill development that you may normally not be comfortable trying.

Steps to a High-Impact Virtual Makerspace

Contrary to what software developers would have you believe, there's more to creating a high-impact virtual makerspace than simply purchasing the latest and greatest products or tech tools. The good news is that it's not as difficult as you might believe either. The following sections detail the five basic steps to creating a successful virtual environment for making:

- Provide a dedicated online space to support maker learning.
- Develop and consistently implement student routines.
- Create and communicate clear learning intentions for every task.
- Scaffold opportunities for connection and collaboration throughout the maker process.
- Go beyond products: Have students document their maker learning process.

Provide a Dedicated Online Space

Establish a dedicated virtual space where students can go to obtain information for each part of the maker learning process. Doing so provides a "one-stop-shop" location where students can locate design challenge resources, see their progress on the multiple steps of the design process, and even showcase final products. This online space can be a specific class in an online learning platform or a workflow tool, such as Google Classroom or Seesaw, where students go to engage in specific steps of the maker learning process. Or you could set up a specific virtual space for your maker work in your learning management system (LMS), such as Canvas, Schoology, or PowerSchool Learning. Even if a specific student maker project is taking place in the context of another subject matter's virtual workspace or LMS course, having a dedicated online space or section to engage students in the specific steps of the design process is valuable. To help students understand what they need to know and do, make sure your online learning spaces provide and organize information in a clear and consistent way. In addition, include tools (such as rubrics and checklists) and opportunities for formal self-reflection to help students gauge their progress in the learning process or the development of a specific skill in relation to the desired end state.

Foster Student Routines

Learners thrive in environments that provide consistency and set routines. Developing routines that outline how and where learners will access specific activities during the design process allows learners to focus on intentional design work and skill development. When constructing directions for students, it is important to organize them in a way that provides specific steps that overtly communicate what a learner needs to know and do. Specifically, learners should be able to use directions not only as a way to accomplish a task but also to use directions to prompt reflection about where they are in relation to what they need to know, specific skills they need to demonstrate, and information they need to develop deeper understanding of. In order to facilitate this process, provide learners with a checklist or steps that allow them to go back over their work, review for completeness, and identify gaps in their learning. Furthermore, anything educators can do to simplify directions, steps, clicks, or time spent trying to decipher a prompt or navigate an online system will allow learners to allocate their efforts toward the more critical elements of the work.

Organize your learning management system or online learning system in a way that models routines and contributes to teacher clarity. Creating a consistent procedure that students are responsible for during each step of the maker process also contributes to learners' ability to develop executive function skills. You can use your online tools to form these routines by creating dedicated spaces within your online learning platform for each phase of the design process. For example: In order to show learning and process, create a specific module, page, or topic that houses all the content, supports, and activities learners need for a specific phase of the design process (Figure 3.1). Depending on your LMS, you may also be able to use specific modules or pages with subpages to support this organization if you are integrating this project into a preexisting online learning management system. For example:

- **GOOGLE CLASSROOM:** Use Topics to organize the maker process. *Topic 3: Prototype Sketch*
- **SEESAW:** Use Folders to organize the maker process. *Folder 1: Research*
- **LEARNING MANAGEMENT SYSTEM:** Use specific modules or pages with subpages to provide dedicated places for each phase of the design process. *Module 1: Interviews & Observations*

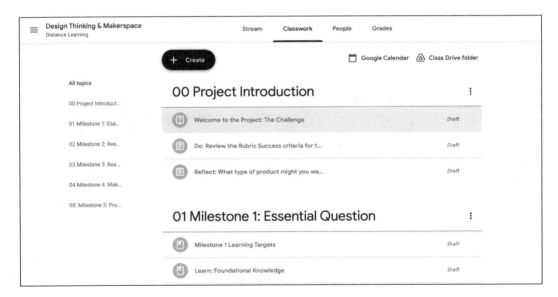

Figure 3.1 Organize your learning management system or online learning system in a way that models routines, contributes to teacher clarity, and helps students navigate the different stages of the design process.

In addition to structuring your online environment by each phase of the design process, create consistent action items that learners must complete during each of these phases. For example, name elements students must produce at each phase of the design process: Documentation, Self-Assessment and Reflection, and Next-Step Goal Setting (Table 3.1). Specifically, these tasks can become routines that focus on helping students to be able to answer the following questions:

- What do I need to know?
- What skills do I need to develop?
- What does it look like to be successful?
- Where am I in my current learning?
- What can I do if I am stuck?
- What do I need to focus on next?
- What do I do if it doesn't work?

TABLE 3.1 Sample Learning Artifacts for Design Process Phases

SAMPLE COMPONENTS	SAMPLE PROMPTS
Documentation For each phase of the design thinking process, have students take photos, take screenshots, or make videos that capture their work in action or the development of their process or product.	Create a Google Slides deck with photos from the _____ phase of your project. Create a screencast explaining your sketch and how your prototype will work. Create an infographic that shares the data you collected from your interviews.

SAMPLE COMPONENTS	SAMPLE PROMPTS
Self-Assessment and Reflection For each phase of the design thinking process, have students engage in self-assessment tasks that require them to review success criteria and rubrics to name evidence from their work that supports where they are in their learning. Provide students opportunities to create reflections that share what they have learned about themselves as learners and what skills they still need to develop.	List success criteria: • What do you see when you look at the details of your work? • Use your rubrics to think about what you did well and what you would want to improve. • How would you make your work better? Goal: What do I need to do to get better at _____? Steps: How do I plan to do this? Evidence: What evidence will show I've achieved my goal? Think about the difference between "poor" work, "good" work, and "great" work. After reviewing the success criteria, what would be an example of how different qualities of work can look? • What do you really understand about _____? • What questions/uncertainties do you still have about _____? • What was the most/least effective in _____? • How could you improve _____? • What would you do differently next time? • What are you most proud of? • What are you most disappointed in? • How difficult was _____ for you? • What are your strengths/weaknesses in _____? • What grade/score do you deserve? Why? • How does what you've learned connect to your other learning? • How has what you've learned changed your thinking? • How does what you've learned relate to the present and future? • What follow-up work is needed?

continues

SAMPLE COMPONENTS	SAMPLE PROMPTS
Next-Step Goal Setting For each phase of the design thinking process, have students engage in goal setting. Providing students with opportunities to identify their current state and develop their next steps is a powerful way to empower student self-efficacy.	Things I need to work on the most: **Your Plan:** Can I do this myself? ☐ Yes ☐ No If no, who could help? Teacher • Other Student _____ • Family Member _____ How likely am I to succeed: ☐ Not Very ☐ Possibly ☐ Likely To get better at _____, I could _____. One thing I am going to start doing is _____. I'll start doing this on _____ (date) and work on it until _____ (date). One way I'll know I'm getting better is _____.

TOOLS TO SUPPORT THIS WORK

- Camera
- Video
- Screencastify
- SoundTrap
- TouchCast
- PDF- and image-annotation tools
- Notes app
- Kami
- Padlet
- Google Forms
- Google Sites
- Explain Everything
- ShowMe
- Flipgrid

Communicate Clear Learning Intentions

One of the most impactful things a teacher can do to improve clarity and support students in focusing on what they need to learn is to create student-friendly learning intentions. This will help students understand the skills or knowledge they need to gain during the process of a specific learning task. When creating content in an online environment or designing specific learning experiences, focus on crafting accessible learning intentions, which is a more valuable use of your time than solely constructing directions for tasks. Whether you are posting an assignment, starting a discussion thread, or creating another type of student learning task, improving your teacher clarity with learning intentions will help students in their ability to focus on the larger goals of student achievement. Table 3.2 includes techniques you can incorporate to increase teacher clarity and student awareness of expectations for learning when constructing a maker learning experience within a virtual environment or when evaluating a current virtual space dedicated to maker learning. To help you assess your efforts in creating high-impact maker learning tasks with clear intentions, you can use a checklist such as Table 3.3, which you can also download from the Chapter 3 resources.

TABLE 3.2 Techniques for Clarity of Expectations in Maker Learning Experiences

TECHNIQUES	SAMPLES
"I Can" Statements Supply statements that students can use to reflect on and check to see if they are successful.	I can sketch my prototype. I can explain how my prototype will work before making it.
Checklists and Rubrics Provide checklists that guide students toward completion and help them decipher "what good looks like" or name what elements must be present for accuracy and completeness.	Checklist: Create a plan to test your prototype: ☐ I have a plan to test if my prototype works. ☐ I know what I need to learn more about. ☐ I am organizing my information. ☐ I made a chart or graph to understand my information. ☐ I know what works and what does not. ☐ I need to meet with my teacher.
Metacognitive and Self-Reflection Tasks When writing directions for students, include tasks that require them to share what they are thinking about or learning. Incorporating opportunities for self-reflection and review of their own work also improves the chances that students catch errors in their work.	I used to think, but now I know... I see, I think, I wonder... What excites me is... What worries me is... What I need to know now is... To move forward I should.... Underline an example of... Circle key words in your response that show where you are in your current work.

TABLE 3.3 Teacher Checklist: Developing High-Impact Virtual Maker Learning Tasks

QUALITIES OF A HIGH-IMPACT VIRTUAL MAKER EXPERIENCE	ANSWER: YES OR NO	COMMENTS: IF *YES*, GIVE EVIDENCE. IF *NO*, HOW WILL YOU REVISE?
The content of the maker experience matches the learning intention.	Does the maker task require the student to use the content or skills specified by the learning intention? Yes _____ No _____	
The cognitive process of the maker experience matches the process of the learning intention.	Does the maker task require the student to use the cognitive process specified by the learning intention? Yes _____ No _____	
The task directions are well organized, and the learning intentions are clear to students.	Would the student know what to do for all aspects of the maker task? Yes _____ No _____	
The directions and learning intentions are clear and cohesive to an adult supporting the student.	Would the parent or adult know what to do for all aspects of the maker task? Yes _____ No _____	
The success criteria for evaluating student work can be used to provide mastery-oriented feedback.	Are the success criteria supplied able to be used for evaluating student work or providing mastery-oriented feedback? Yes _____ No _____	

Scaffold Opportunities for Connection and Collaboration

Provide and scaffold opportunities for learners to make thinking visible, physically move ideas around, and provide the space to work in collaborative and co-working settings. Learners may not be able to articulate what they need or illustrate where they are in their progress. The strategies, prompts, and accountable talk stems listed in Table 3.4 can facilitate learners in developing expert learner behaviors and skills that are transferable to a variety of learning environments.

TABLE 3.4 Strategies to Cultivate Expert Learners

STRATEGIES	TOOLS	IMPLEMENTATION TIPS
Create opportunities to connect with other makers in and outside of the classroom.	• Videoconferencing tools • Collaborative documents • Padlet	Provide accountable talk stems and checklists that students use during meetings with peers or teachers so that students can easily reference them.

Sample Student-Accountable Talk Stems:
- I wonder...
- I noticed...
- I liked...
- I feel...
- I can infer...
- My favorite part was...
- An important point was...
- I realized...
- I think...
- The prototype made me think of...
- If I could change something, I would...
- The maker's purpose may be...

Physically move ideas around.	• Interactive whiteboard tools (Zoom, Google Meet, WebEx Whiteboard) • Seesaw Draw feature • Padlet • Post-It App • Google Jamboard	Provide options that allow students to engage in brainstorming using physical and digital tools. Offer options for students to construct ideas using handwriting, drawing, and imagery. Provide options for students to share these creations with and receive feedback from others.

Sample Prompts for Students:
- Create a slideshow of photos that reflect the work you did during this part of the design process.
- Draw a picture or write symbols that summarize your interview findings.
- Write as many words as come to mind to describe who you are solving a problem for.
- Draw a picture to help you remember as much as you can about _____.
- Take your photo, and then use the Markup tool to write what you are thinking.
- Use a storyboard to show the steps you will take to make your prototype.
- Use a storyboard to show the steps you will take to test your prototype.
- Draw a picture of who you are making for.

continues

STRATEGIES	TOOLS	IMPLEMENTATION TIPS
Make thinking visible and audible.	Flipgrid iMovie Trailers Google Forms Google Docs Infographic tools Canva Camera tools Screencasting tools	Provide options for students to document physical and digital creations during various stages of the design process. Create opportunities for students to share what they are learning, what they are wondering, and what they are struggling with. Engage students in specific questions to share their thinking.

Sample Prompts for Students:
- What did you notice?
- What did you like?
- What is your opinion?
- What did you wonder?
- What does this mean?
- What did you learn?
- How did it make you feel?
- Which parts, if any, did you especially like? Explain your thinking.
- What did you read or see that makes you think that?
- What do you know that you didn't know before?
- Which parts, if any, would you have changed if you were the designer or maker?

Document the Maker Learning Process

It is important for students to be able to tell the story of their learning. Creating opportunities for students to document the steps of their design process improves their ability to manage the pace of their work. Providing students with a timeline and choices for how they can document and share the steps they are completing during the design process also develops progress-monitoring skills. Allow students to use a variety of digital tools to capture their design process; providing them opportunities for personalization is empowering. Table 3.5 suggests ways to assign required elements while still offering students opportunities to personalize their design process and share their work. Student portfolios can be assigned to individual students or to groups of students. If you choose to have students create group portfolios, it can be helpful to assign specific roles for each student in the group so they clearly understand what content they are responsible for in the collective portfolio.

STEPS TO A HIGH-IMPACT VIRTUAL MAKERSPACE

TABLE 3.5 Sample Design Portfolio

DESIGN PORTFOLIO ELEMENTS	INDIVIDUAL	GROUP
Introduction to the Assignment	*Incorporate the following content into your portfolio.*	*Group members will work to collaboratively incorporate the following elements into the collective portfolio. To increase accountability, assign specific elements to individual group members.*
Element 1: Meet the Maker(s)	Photo or video and description of the final product	Photo or video and description of the final product
Element 2: Subject Matter and User Testing	• State the problem and list/identify the target audience. • Provide a description for the product. • Share photos or notes from research and information gathered.	• State the problem and list/identify the target audience. • Provide a description for the product. • Share photos or notes from research and information gathered. • Summary Reflection: What did you learn in your role during this project?
Element 3: Visualize the Design Process	• Visualize *each phase* of the design—from sketching to advanced sketching to photos of the different stages of prototypes. • Summarize what materials were used for making the prototype and *why* they were selected. • Provide a summary of how the prototype works (can be on the sketch).	• Visualize *each phase* of the design—from sketching to advanced sketching to photos of the different stages of prototypes. • Summarize what materials were used for making the prototype and *why* they were selected. • Provide a summary of how the prototype works (can be on the sketch). • Summary Reflection: What did you learn in your role during this project?
Element 4: Reflection and Progress Updates	*Either write or create a video reflection on the following:* • What was the most interesting thing you learned during the process? • How will you leverage design thinking in the future?	• Summary of where the team is at the end of each class period on the site. • "Today we accomplished:" Complete one to three sentences for each day. • Photo(s) of the team's work in action for each day. • Team materials/handouts resources and links or embedded photos on the site of the process. • Summary Reflection: What did you learn in your role during this project?

UDL in Your Maker Learning Environment

Have you ever experienced a situation that was so daunting you decided it wasn't worth your time? Perhaps you gave up. Perhaps you trudged ahead but swore you would never do it again. Now imagine that you're a student and that daunting situation is your learning experience. It's a scenario none of us like to contemplate—and one we can avoid. We want all learners to be unencumbered, motivated, and willing to take calculated risks and act strategically. Built around the three principles of Engagement, Representation, and Action and Expression, the Universal Design for Learning Guidelines can be leveraged to create personalized and authentic experiences for students that will help them grow to be expert learners (CAST, 2018).

Physical and virtual makerspaces, in turn, provide an opportunity to model, encourage, and maximize the implementation of the Universal Design for Learning (UDL) Guidelines. Although the UDL Guidelines are not prescriptive, they do provide a vertical dimension that addresses three critical layers—Access, Build, and Internalize—that assist in removing barriers to learning (CAST, 2018). These three layers are a powerful ladder for increasing access to learning, shaping how learners build understanding, and supporting how they internalize learning behaviors that are critical for thriving and self-regulating in familiar as well as novel situations. These vertical layers of alignment also offer educators a direction for how to go about constructing opportunities, environments, and experiences that propel students forward in their growth.

Focused on each of the UDL principles individually, the sections that follow outline best practices, protocols, and resources that improve accessibility and boost students' executive functioning skills. In addition, you'll find strategies for guiding educator and learner usage of the makerspace and helping students be more productive, as well as concrete examples that model the implementation of the UDL Guidelines within maker learning experiences, makerspaces, and design studios. Putting these resources to work also will reduce the amount of pre-planning teachers have to do before bringing students into the space.

Resources for Engagement

Have you ever had students working together but not collaborating effectively? Have you ever had students participating in a peer-review process, where the exchange around mastery-oriented feedback was thin? Or have you ever outlined the steps in a process, yet students seem to still get lost or off task? All of these scenarios exemplify a lack of engagement. Even with intentional teacher planning, sometimes students are still at risk of disengagement.

Engagement is proportional to a student's ability to decipher what they need to know and do to be successful and to feel that they have the self-efficacy to accomplish that specific goal. From maker-specific accountable talk stems, to methods for fostering self-regulation and meaningful collaboration, the resources in this section will model and share strategies that can help all learners reach higher levels of engagement. Specifically, the resources that follow are designed to help learners:

○ Regulate their own learning (Resources 3.1–3.3)

○ Sustain effort and motivation (Resources 3.4–3.6)

○ Find options that engage and interest them (Resources 3.7–3.9)

while also addressing the questions:

○ How will learners engage in the makerspace or maker learning environment?

○ How will learners engage in maker learning?

RESOURCE 3.1: SELF-REGULATION CHARTS

Providing a dedicated place and process where students can indicate how they are feeling about the work they are doing provides opportunities for students to engage in meta-cognitive self-reflection. Self-Regulation Charts allow students to express how they are feeling about the process of their work (Figure 3.2). Have students write their name on the back of a sticky note and place it on the chart. Then when you are taking them off, take note of the names and where individual students are at. Take a photo of the sticky notes before removing them so you can revisit them later or have students reflect on any changes in the process. Gathering this information allows you to quickly gain insight into how students are feeling about their progress and plan next steps for personalized and whole group support.

CHAPTER 3: INTEGRATE UDL GUIDELINES INTO MAKER EXPERIENCES

Figure 3.2 Self-regulation charts that are highly visual can be useful for non-reading students as well as offer variability in the ways students are able to share their perceptions of their progress and learning.

TABLE 3.6 Virtual Variations: Self-Regulation Charts

TIPS	TOOLS TO USE
Keep it simple.	• Padlet
• Flipgrid
• Pages
• Book Creator
• Google Slides
• Keynote
• Videoconferencing, livestreaming tools
Offer opportunities for students to share their feelings on interactive boards that provide choice for digital content.	
Ask students to reflect on self-regulation by having them keep journals.	
During livestreaming meetings, have students hold up a representation of how they are feeling about their work. You could provide students with emojis they can print or ask them to draw their feelings.	

RESOURCE 3.2: SHARED WORK AGREEMENTS

Shared Work Agreements help learners set the stage for self-regulation. Specifically, have students create shared work agreements around makerspace safety, collaboration, brainstorming, and sharing feedback (Figure 3.3). Asking students to create these rather than providing them with a readymade list increases the ownership students can take with this work. It also makes it easier for students to describe and articulate what authentic examples of student behaviors could look like in their learning environment. Table 3.7 offers tips and tools for creating shared work agreements.

Figure 3.3 Make Shared Work Agreement prompts easy to access and assign to different groups of students. This will increase the likelihood that teachers will engage students in these types of thinking prompts.

CHAPTER 3: INTEGRATE UDL GUIDELINES INTO MAKER EXPERIENCES

TABLE 3.7 Virtual Variations: Shared Work Agreements

TIPS	TOOLS TO USE
Make it interactive.	• Padlet
Offer opportunities for students to co-create shared work agreements.	• Google Docs
	• Google Slides
During livestreaming meetings, use breakout features for students to create a visual representation or construct their shared work agreements.	• Videoconferencing, livestreaming, breakout rooms

RESOURCE 3.3: SPACE CONFIGURATIONS GUIDE

To ensure your makerspace is an agile learning space, create a Space Configurations Guide that names and illustrates with images how various areas of your space can be or are intended to be used. Such guides can help educators and learners maximize how they use makerspace furniture and space within the room to respond to learner needs and provide choice within the makerspace.

STOP & JOT

What might you do to create more flexibility and agility within learning spaces?

Naming and visualizing models for intentional use of space can assist educators and students in making the most of the space you have available (Figure 3.4). For example, the spaces described in David Thornburg's "Campfires in Cyberspace" (2007) and Prakash Nair's *Blueprint for Tomorrow: Redesigning Schools for Student-Centered Learning* (2014) use highly visual naming conventions: Campfire, Cave, Watering Whole, and Wilderness. These naming conventions not only can capture students' attention and imagination but also lead to more purposeful discussions about how they can help accomplish certain types of work. Having intentional discussions with students and modeling specific strategies for how to create agile learning spaces teach students about the ways they can act strategically within a learning space.

"Campfire." The space: offers presentation area and ability for small groups to gather to share ideas.

"Cave." The space: allows for introspective learning, with resources to help students reflect.

"Watering Hole." The space: provides options for small groups to work together on developing a prototype.

"Wilderness." The space: allows for learning by doing.

Figure 3.4 Help stakeholders maximize how learning spaces are used by providing visuals that represent configuration of the space and use of resources. Include imagery that helps them to understand the larger purpose of that configuration and use of the learning space.

RESOURCE 3.4: ACCOUNTABLE TALK CARDS

Accountable Talk Cards offer specific sentence stems that guide students through high-impact feedback and collaboration (Figure 3.5). Providing learners with accountable talk stems models ways to start highly effective collaborative dialogues. In addition, sentence stems also provide learners with prompting to organize their thinking. It is also important to provide accountable talk stems that incorporate elements of the mastery-oriented feedback or success criteria that you need learners to demonstrate proficiency in their final or revised work. Sometimes students just don't have the right words to start a powerful dialogue with peers, and accountable talk

Figure 3.5 Provide students with specific sentence stems that guide them through high-impact feedback and collaboration.

Accountable Talk Card- Prototype Testing	
Observation/ Conclusions	**What is working...**
My test shows ____ because ____	I see ____
Think my results are ____ because ____	What is working well with my prototype testing is ____
Clarification	**What is Working**
What problem does your prototype solve?	What I think is working well is ____
Explain more please...	According to my observations ____
What is your evidence?	I know ____ because ____
Confusion	**Extension**
I don't understand ____	I would like to add ____
I'm confused about ____	I wonder ____
	Next time you might want to test ____
	I would like to add ____ to improve my prototype or design

Accountable Talk Card- General	
Agreement	**Disagreement**
I agree with ____ because ____	I disagree with ____ because ____
	I'm not sure I agree with what ____ said
I like what ____ said because ____	because ____
Clarification	**Confirmation**
Can you give me an example?	When I read ____ it said ____
Explain more please...	According to my observations ____
What is your evidence?	I know ____ because
Confusion	**Extension**
I don't understand ____	I would like to add ____
I'm confused about ____	I wonder ____
	I would like to add on to what ____ said

stems on readily available cards can also boost student confidence. Providing students with Accountable Talk Cards that are designed intentionally to guide students in the evaluation and testing of prototypes is helpful. (Downloadable examples are available in the Chapter 3 resources.)

RESOURCE 3.5: CLEAN-UP JOB CARDS

Avoid student distractions by creating cards that detail clear job descriptions that facilitate how to categorize and organize materials during cleanup. Be sure to use text and images. The text lists provide structure for organizing resources, while the cards' visuals make it easy for nonreaders to take action as well (Figure 3.6).

Figure 3.6 Tangible cards that outline specific tasks for cleaning up the makerspace or maker materials help keep students on task when transitioning out of the makerspace or activity.

RESOURCE 3.6: ACTION-INSPIRING SIGNAGE

Provide signage in your makerspace to guide learners in keeping their creations organized. Including visual cues is a powerful way to help learners know how to use the space most appropriately, increasing safety and maximizing resources (Figure 3.7). In addition, these visuals can be used for teachers to reference at any given time and assist in directing or redirecting students. Clean, simple signage that includes graphics can help students infer meaning as well. Canva is a great design tool for creating powerful signage, and it enables you to download your signs in several file types.

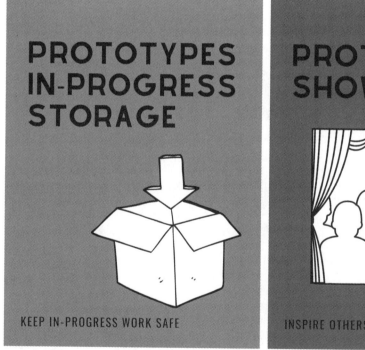

Figure 3.7 Signage does not have to be elaborate to be effective. Create visuals that provide students with direction and facilitate organization.

RESOURCE 3.7: CHOICE AUDITORY AND MOVEMENT BREAKS

There are different reasons to step away from a task at various times. Sometimes you may be working in an overstimulating environment, such as makerspaces can be at times. Other times you need a moment to clear your head and return to a problem with a fresh mind. Providing time and space for students to take a break from extra noise, to get away from commotion, and to regroup if needed helps students develop a heightened sense of self-awareness and their ability to self-regulate. Because makerspaces are busy places, have a moveable sign that can be used to designate a location where students can go to take a short time away from noise, overstimulation, or a difficult situation (Figure 3.8). Teachers can decide when and where to dedicate this type of area and work with students to create appropriate use guidelines and norms. Another suggestion is to include a general expectation about how long the breaks typically should be and when it is most appropriate to use. Pro Tip: Prior to working in the makerspace, engage students in creating a collaborative work agreement about when and how to appropriately monitor sound as well as other modes of communication in the makerspace (see Resource 3.2).

Figure 3.8 Minimize the impacts of an overstimulating environment with pop-up signage for designated sound or moment breaks.

RESOURCE 3.8: AT-A-GLANCE GUIDE TO MAKERSPACE CONTENT

Your makerspace will be stocked with a variety of tools, technologies, and capacities to support personalized design projects, all of which students can access when making prototypes. Provide an At-a-Glance Guide to your makerspace's contents (Figure 3.9) to help educators and learners get the most out of the space and support individualized interests. Further, depending on the type of design challenge and prototypes students will be making, you may want to engage students in a conversation about what type of materials they might be looking for, having them reflect on the materials they think they will need and where to find them.

Figure 3.9 Having a Makerspace Resources At-a-Glance Guide can help students take a more strategic approach to identifying the materials they want to use for prototyping.

At-A-Glance Guide to Maker Materials

Purpose: The purpose of this guide is to help educators and learners become familiar with common maker tasks and resources they have access to in the makerspaces.

Maker Learner Task	Recommended Tools
Brainstorming/ Ideation	❏ Post-it Notes ❏ Markers/Highlighters ❏ Chart Paper ❏ Dry Erase Boards ❏ Colored Pencils ❏ Paper/Construction Paper
Coding/ Programming	❏ Spheros ❏ Dash/ Cue ❏ Ozobots ❏ Makey Makey
Rapid Prototyping	❏ Cardboard ❏ MakeDos ❏ Foil/Filters ❏ Foam ❏ Fasteners ❏ Cutters
Maker Technologies	❏ Robots ❏ Greenscreen ❏ Microphones ❏ iPads/Tripods/iPad Cases ❏ iPad Remote ❏ iPad Creation Apps

RESOURCE 3.9: GETTING TO KNOW THE MAKERSPACE WALKABOUT ACTIVITY

The Getting to Know the Makerspace Walkabout Activity enables educators and learners to familiarize themselves with the space and resources while supporting individualized interests (Figure 3.10). This is a great activity to help students be more mindful of how they are using resources in the makerspace and develop executive functioning skills necessary for organizing and planning project work.

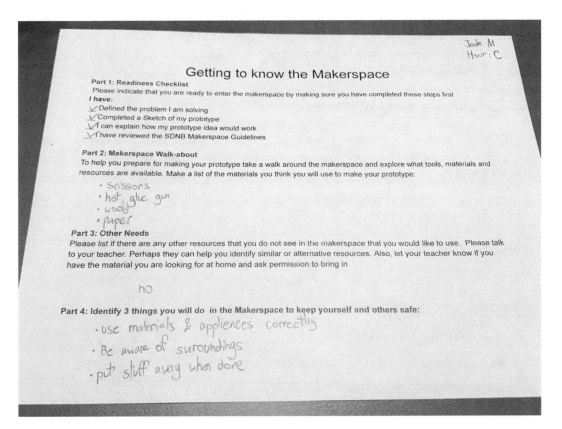

Figure 3.10 A structured tour of your makerspace and its resources will help students organize and plan their project work, as well as be more mindful of how they use resources.

Resources for Representation

Have you ever found yourself trying to cook dinner but feeling like you are spending more time puzzling over a specific action step in the recipe or the ingredients you need for a step than you are spending completing the step's actions? Or maybe you started to read that recipe but got so discouraged you skipped it. More often than not, learners find themselves in a similar situation when it comes to perceiving and understanding a specific task or expectation at hand. I find that one of the most overlooked yet highly powerful components to setting learners up for success falls under teacher clarity.

Sometimes, it's about finding ways to chunk information so it's more digestible and makes it easy for learners to recognize patterns, critical features, big ideas, or relationships. Other times it's about organizing information in a way that makes it easier for learners to focus on demonstrating what they need to know and do, versus trying to decode what the directions are saying.

In this section, you will find resources and strategies that are designed to increase learner stamina, motivation, and deeper understanding based on how information is perceived and comprehended.

Specifically, the resources that follow will help you ensure your makerspace provides options that help all learners:

- Reach deeper understanding of design thinking (Resources 3.10, 3.11)
- Understand symbols and tools (Resources 3.12, 3.13)
- Perceive what needs to be learned (Resources 3.14, 3.15)

while also addressing the questions:

- How is the makerspace presented to all learners?
- How are maker learning tasks presented to all learners?

RESOURCE 3.10: GRAB-AND-GO CHECK FOR UNDERSTANDING CARDS

Check for Understanding Cards encourage options for students to make their current thinking visible. Keep a large variety of these grab-and-go cards easily accessible in your makerspace; teachers are more likely to employ this method of formative assessment if the cards are on hand, organized, and require no additional preparation (Figure 3.11). In order to make it easier for teachers to navigate the provided cards, keep them in one place, perhaps using different colored baskets to signify the type of thinking or topics they align with. It is also very helpful to number the baskets and provide a general sheet that shows the number and corresponding prompt so teachers can easily locate the exact Check for Understanding Card they are looking for.

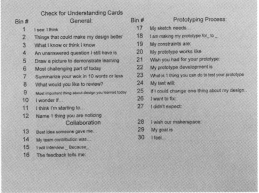

Figure 3.11 Create systematic ways to organize Check for Understanding Cards and provide a guide to help educators easily find the cards they are looking for.

RESOURCE 3.11: GATHERING STUDENT CHECK FOR UNDERSTANDING CARD RESPONSES

Give each makerspace signage and a dedicated place for learners to submit their Check for Understanding Cards (Figure 3.12). Even something as simple as signage serves as a powerful reminder to educators about the assessment resources available in your space and during the design process. You could also use Google Forms to collect student responses to the Check for Understanding Cards in a spreadsheet, making the data you collect easier to sort and visualize. If specific Check for Understanding prompts are transposed into a sample form, educators can easily make a copy of the original Google Forms file and personalize it. These digital versions make it easier for teachers to implement and for students to fill out more frequently. In addition, Google Forms enables you to add images and other multimedia to questions and response options, providing more options for students to share their thinking other than using text; for example, students can respond by creating an artifact in another program or upload handwritten or sketched responses. Table 3.8 offers tips and tools for creating response options.

Figure 3.12 Specific signage provides visual cues to help students know where to turn in their Check for Understanding responses when they are done.

TABLE 3.8 Virtual Variations: Grab-and-Go Check for Understanding Responses

TIPS	TOOLS TO USE
Create and share video reflections to the Check for Understanding prompt.	• Flipgrid • Clips
Post a response to the Check for Understanding prompt in a shared space.	• Padlet • Numbers • Google Jamboard • Collaborative documents
Easily collect and organize student responses for teacher review.	• Google Forms • SoGoSurvey

RESOURCE 3.12: STUDENT COLLABORATIVE GROUP CARD

Shared makerspaces can be very busy places with lots of users. To make the most of the time different classes have in the makerspace, stock your makerspace with Student Collaborative Group cards. These are physical cards or signage that designate where students need to be at a given time and help direct students when a teacher is dividing a class into collaborative working groups. Use vibrant colors, specific shapes, and numbers as well as words to help learners understand where they need to be and who they are working with (Figure 3.13). Pro Tip: Place the cards in different places within the makerspace or student work area to help groups organize where they are working based on the task at hand.

Figure 3.13 Providing colorful physical cards that include images and numbers can help students navigate their assignments and group work efficiently. This is exceptionally helpful in a busy, free-flowing place such as the makerspace.

RESOURCE 3.13: CATEGORIZE MATERIALS IN THE SPACE

Categorize materials in your makerspace by adding specific signage and assigning labels to help students navigate how to best use and conserve resources within the makerspace (Figure 3.14). Some materials in your makerspace will be one-time use or consumable; others will be semi-consumable, meaning that they can be used and re-used to a certain state, and others are non-consumable and can be used multiple times in many different ways. It is important to help learners differentiate between the different types and uses of materials in the makerspace. In some cases, after a project it may be appropriate to take apart prototypes and repurpose the materials used. Finding ways to label the various types of materials can also help with maximizing the use of resources and assist in future planning and budgeting for needed materials.

Figure 3.14 Guide learners in acting strategically with a specific resource or material by assigning specific images, colors, and categories to the various types of materials in the makerspace.

RESOURCE 3.14: MAKING LEARNING INTENTIONS VISIBLE

Create a dedicated place in your makerspace for educators to post the learning intention of the day and guide learners working in the space (Figure 3.15). You can use specific signs that signal where the learning intentions are posted to engage learners in conversations about what they need to accomplish and where they are in the process. If you are working in a virtual makerspace or a physical makerspace with a virtual component, be sure to have learning intentions accessible throughout the design process. Encourage learners to take time to reflect on where they are in relation to the learning intention and identify what gaps might exist. Certain workflow tools and apps such as Seesaw allow teachers to provide audio directions along with text, as well as include imagery or symbols if desired. This can be a powerful way to help all students consistently engage with learning intentions.

Figure 3.15 Encourage learners to take time to reflect on where they are in relation to the learning intention and identify what gaps might exist.

RESOURCE 3.15: DESIGN THINKING PROCESS SIGNAGE

Because there are numerous steps in the design thinking process, it is important to provide opportunities for learners to build their understanding of each distinct step. One way to do this is to use wall space in your makerspace to post the steps of the process. These visuals should include details and graphics that help students develop their understanding of the steps. Adding signage provides an opportunity to help educators and learners focus on and gain awareness of the specific elements of the design process (Figure 3.16). Encourage teachers to point, cue, and reference each step in the design process as students are engaged in them.

Figure 3.16 Display signage that helps students visualize steps of the design process and what important skills are used during those steps.

Resources for Action and Expression

When I was in fourth grade, I broke two fingers on my right hand. I vividly remember my hot pink cast and the problem it posed in school, because I was right-handed. This was long before 1:1 computing, mobile learning technologies, or voice to text. Specifically, I remember the physical feeling of stress I had: How was I going to write down the words on the paper for the weekly science vocabulary quiz?

My mother expressed my concerns to the teacher, and she had agreed to provide me with an alternative option. What a relief! When quiz time arrived, however, the teacher told me she was going to read the quiz questions aloud to me, and I would write down the answers. Relief turned back to internal panic, and I did the best I could to record my answers on paper with my less-than-effective left hand. It probably also didn't help that this was a time and place where "good students" were compliant and didn't push back or ask too many questions, even in the case of self-advocacy and acting strategically as a learner.

Although clearly my limitations in fourth grade were physical and situational, the biggest takeaway from the story is that there are multiple ways learners can demonstrate skills, knowledge, and understanding. This is even more feasible today, given the prevalence of technology and opportunities for learners to choose from a variety of mediums to demonstrate learning. In this section, you will find strategies such as Target Storming brainstorming techniques, guides for developing digital portfolios, and methods for displaying student work to model and inspire others. Providing makers with opportunities to demonstrate their authentic solutions and prototypes using a variety of mediums and methodologies is at the core of the Action and Expression principle of UDL.

The resources that follow will help you ensure that your makerspace provides options that help all learners:

- Act strategically (Resources 3.16, 3.17)
- Express themselves fluently (Resource 3.18)
- Physically respond (Resource 3.19)

while also addressing the questions:

- How are learners expected to act strategically and express themselves in the makerspace?
- How are learners expected to act strategically and express themselves in maker learning?

RESOURCE 3.16: STUDENT PORTFOLIOS

Student Portfolios enable learners to document by doing, and they can create portfolios with a variety of tools (Figure 3.17). Learners can create digital portfolios to document their personalized process, works, and artifacts with images, videos, text, or any combination of media. Be sure to provide students with templates that allow them to capture their work in personalized ways. Encourage students to take photos and make video reflections while they are at various stages of the maker learning process, for example. Google Sites, Adobe Spark, and Apple Pages offer dynamic ways for students to capture their process.

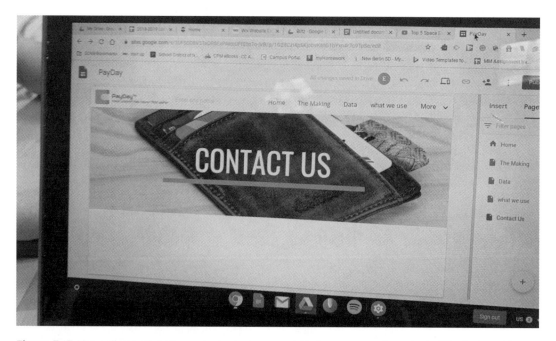

Figure 3.17 Use online tools to have students document their process and product with photos, video reflections, and more from various stages of the maker learning process.

RESOURCE 3.17: TARGET STORMING ACTIVITY

The idea of the Target Storming activity is to help students evaluate their brainstorming ideas. Provide each group with a sheet of chart paper on which to draw a target; the outer ring will hold "alright" ideas, the middle for "pretty good," and the bullseye for the "most viable/favorite" ideas. Students then write or sketch their ideas on Post-it Notes (or smaller pieces of paper) and decide which target ring to add them to (Figure 3.18). Providing learners with an opportunity to sketch or digitally construct representations of their ideas versus just writing them provides more opportunities for learners to express their thinking in a modality that is most effective for them. Pro Tip: Students can also create digital cards for this activity; see Table 3.9 for more ideas.

Figure 3.18 Transform a paper storyboard into sketch cards to more easily share and move ideas around.

TABLE 3.9 Virtual Variations: Target Storming Activity

TIPS	TOOLS TO USE
Create visualizations of ideas.	• Google Slides • Pollunit.com • Google Jamboard • Videoconferencing whiteboard features
Share and move ideas around.	• Padlet • Google Jamboard • Post-it App
Sort, vote, and evaluate ideas.	• Dotstorming.com • Padlet • Pollunit.com

RESOURCE 3.18: STUDENT WORK SHOWCASE

Use makerspace signage that highlights opportunities to showcase student work and to engage students in conversations about peer design (Figure 3.19). You can also increase student agency by allowing students to choose the modality that they think is most appropriate for showcasing their work. After all, makerspaces offer options for creating and displaying work digitally as well as physically! Makerspaces should provide a variety of capacities for students to express themselves and inspire others through their showcased work. For example, you could use the Check for Understanding Cards (Resource 3.10) to spark observations about peer work.

TIP: In order to increase accessibility, enable the closed captioning feature in Google Slides when in Present mode. This will provide your audience with live closed captioning during your presentation.

Figure 3.19 Create a dedicated space or time for students to showcase their work in real time or asynchronously.

UDL IN YOUR MAKER LEARNING ENVIRONMENT

RESOURCE 3.19: APPROPRIATE USE GUIDELINES FOR MAKERSPACES

Makerspaces provide students with a variety of spaces and choice for sitting, standing, recording, building, and much more. In addition to using the Space Configuration Guide (Resources 3.6–3.10) to inspire how learners choose to use your active learning spaces, you can post Appropriate Use Guidelines to support educators and learners as they prepare to enter the makerspace. To improve accessibility of your guidelines, create multiple versions of grade-band-friendly language for students (Figure 3.20). You can also leverage makerspace Appropriate Use Guidelines and Maker Manifestos as contracts that learners review with the educator and sign prior to engaging in the space.

TIP: In addition to highly visual signage, incorporate QR codes that link to video or auditory versions of the information being presented. AI-enabled voice readers and text-to-speech tools increase opportunities for making the most of physical signage while providing more opportunities for learner voice and choice.

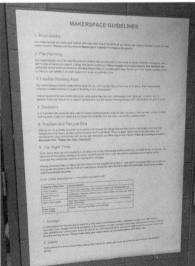

Figure 3.20 Post Makerspace Guidelines and Appropriate Use Recommendations in places that are easy for students to review and reference. You can even turn such resources into personalized learning contracts.

Next Steps

Chapter 3 Resources

- Develop clear learning intentions to kick off each phase of the design and maker process.
- Identify appropriate tools for supporting virtual maker and design experiences.
- Use virtual spaces as a way to help students form specific learning behaviors and routines when they are working in virtual or face-to-face environments.
- Integrate ongoing and consistent opportunities for students to engage in goal setting and self-reflection throughout the design process.
- Identify tools and formats to support the use of student portfolios that allow students to document the process of their work as well as the products from each stage.
- Identify and provide specific elements and resources within the makerspace to gain new knowledge of maker tools and techniques, increase motivation, and guide students so they can act in strategic ways.
- Scan the Chapter 3 Resources QR code to check out useful links, templates, and resources for this chapter.

Reflection

After reading Chapter 3, take some time to consider how its ideas apply within your context using the questions below.

- What are three ideas you have for integrating the Universal Design for Learning Guidelines within the maker learning process, resources, or makerspaces?
- What are three characteristics of powerful learning intentions that differentiate them from task or assignment directions?
- Which methods and tools would best help students when they are engaged in the design thinking and maker learning process in virtual, face-to-face, or blended learning environments?

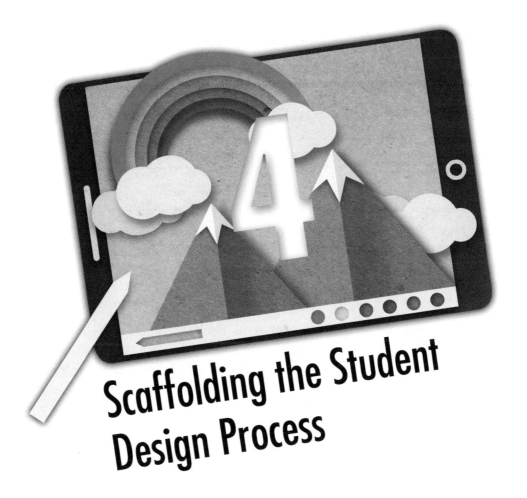

Scaffolding the Student Design Process

By the end of this chapter, you will:

- Evaluate a variety of instructional strategies that can be used to scaffold the student design process.

- Gain multiple methods students can use at specific phases of the design process to self-assess the development of their skills, knowledge, and dispositions.

- Have access to strategies that increase cognitive engagement and metacognition during the design and maker learning process.

Strategies for Each Phase of the Design Process

Building on Chapter 3, this chapter provides educators a variety of strategies that support learners as they work through the stages of the design process. Specifically, the strategies within this chapter are intended to provide dynamic opportunities for students to engage with new learning and share their authentic outcomes at each phase of the design thinking process. Each strategy is aligned to the ISTE Standards for Students and can be used with any number of students via digital tools or low-tech methods. Remember, though, that leveraging digital tools and practices to implement these strategies creates more opportunities for students to maximize accessibility features and increases the strategies' collaborative nature.

The duration of each activity can vary based on the unique needs of learners and the steps you choose to take in scaffolding the learning process. When evaluating how many strategies to employ, consider the unique needs of your learners and choose strategies that best scaffold and fit their needs as well as curriculum schedules. Downloadable graphic organizer templates are available for each of the chapter's strategies; simply scan the Chapter 4 Resources QR code.

As you'll see the strategies are organized into sections based on the stages of the design process (see the "Design Process Key Terms" sidebar). Each section provides you with multiple options and methods for addressing specific student skill development, for example:

- **UNPACKING THE DESIGN CHALLENGE:** Strategies for building foundational knowledge and academic vocabulary, developing brainstorming skills, and preparing for research

- **IDENTIFYING A TARGET USER OR AUDIENCE:** Strategies to sharpen observation and interview skills, as well as methods for collecting and visualizing data

- **RESEARCH AND DEFINE:** Strategies focused on synthesizing information, identifying patterns and trends, and developing problem statements

- **DEFINING PROBLEMS AND IDEATING SOLUTIONS:** Strategies to engage learners in using initial research to define a specific problem to focus on and then ideate possible solutions

- **SKETCHING:** Strategies to support student sketching and prototype planning

DESIGN THINKING PROCESS KEY TERMS

Any new endeavor is likely to have its own specialized terminology, and the design process (Figure 4.1) is no different. Not only do they describe the stages of a typical design challenge, but the following terms also represent common themes embedded throughout the ISTE Innovative Designer standard.

- **EMPATHIZE:** Using the design challenge, and focusing on human need, find out as much information as possible associated with the challenge.

- **DEFINE:** Synthesize that information into patterns and trends. Use these to develop a problem statement that guides action. This may be in the form of a "How might we...?" statement.

- **IDEATE:** Generate ideas. These are the raw materials or digital tools for the development of the prototype.

- **PROTOTYPE:** Assemble ideas into a plausible solution or solutions.

- **EVALUATE:** Test the solution, improve, iterate, and retest (the gray arrows in Figure 4.1 represent this cycle). Continue to reach an effective solution.

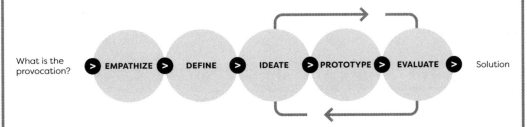

Figure 4.1 While the design thinking process is commonly portrayed as a set of linear steps, it also represents a process that is iterative (as the gray arrows show) and can be adapted to fit a specific design challenge.

If you need to take a deeper dive into these themes, IDEO U (**ideou.com/pages/design-thinking#process**) offers a variety of resources that can be useful for expanding, visualizing, and gaining a deeper understanding of how the design thinking process can be implemented to facilitate creative problem-solving.

- **PROTOTYPING:** Strategies for assembling ideas into plausible solutions
- **EVALUATION:** Strategies for testing solutions, improving concepts, and iterating to develop effective solutions

The strategies that follow dig into the details of each of these phases. For an overview of the full design journey in the form of a useful template, see The Maker Roadmap in Chapter 6 (Figure 6.8, downloadable from the Chapter 6 resources). In addition to helping students keep on track, consistently revisiting a roadmap such as this during their design work journey can help students boost their executive function skills.

HOW-TO STRATEGIES:
Unpacking the Design Challenge

In Chapter 1, we discussed the importance of teacher clarity when designing a maker challenge. With the strategies in this section, you can set students up for success by helping them build the necessary foundational knowledge to enter into a design challenge. Whether you are interested in helping students become more familiar with design thinking or want to build academic vocabulary and ideation skills, you'll find a strategy to help.

STRATEGY 4.1: TEACHING KEY DESIGN TERMS

DURATION OF ACTIVITY: 30–45 minutes

This strategy focuses on building learner vocabulary. Vocabulary development will assist students in the initial steps of the research process as well as to dive deeper into the challenge itself.

WHEN TO USE

The Teaching Key Design Terms strategy works best at the beginning of the project and exploration to help students increase their academic vocabulary as well as to become more familiar with the maker design process.

ALIGNED ISTE STANDARDS FOR STUDENTS
- Innovative Designer, 4a

HOW-TO STRATEGIES: UNPACKING THE DESIGN CHALLENGE   107

> **GO REMOTE**
> - Google Jamboard, Google Slides, Keynote, or Microsoft PowerPoint provide ways for students to work collaboratively or individually during this activity. Assign one term per board or slide to help students stay organized when they are completing the steps of the project. For example, assign each student a specific slide or board where they will complete the steps of the activity.
> - Tools such as Flipgrid and Seesaw, as well as cameras and screencasting features on mobile devices, provide students with options to communicate and reflect on their current level of understanding.

WHAT TO DO

STEP 1: Provide students key terms with corresponding definitions or descriptions. These can be key terms related to the specific design challenge they are about to embark on, as well as the design process in general. No matter how you decide to have students construct their responses, provide a scale (Figure 4.2) that they can use to identify their level of understanding of specific terms. This scale can be used before and after the activity to help students reflect on their learning.

KNOWLEDGE LEVEL	DESCRIPTION
Level 4	I understand even more about the term than I was taught.
Level 3	I understand the term, and I am not confused about any part of what it means.
Level 2	I am a little uncertain about what the term means, but I have a general idea.
Level 1	I am very uncertain about the term. I do not understand what it means.

Figure 4.2 Students can use a scale to identify their level of understanding of specific terms. You can also have students come back to this scale later and compare how their understanding has changed over time.

STEP 2: Ask students to restate the description or definition in their own words.

STEP 3: Ask students to construct a picture, symbols, or graphic representing the term. You can also offer students the option to use photos they find online that they think capture the meaning of the term. (Scan the Chapter 4 Resources QR code for a sample template to help students organize their work for this task.)

STEP 4: Engage students periodically in activities that help them add to their knowledge of these or unfamiliar terms through the design process. This is an activity that can be used in ongoing ways through the process.

STEP 5: Periodically ask students to discuss and revisit these terms with one another. Using digital tools to engage in this activity and keep track of their charts also provides opportunities for students to continue to deepen their understanding and revisit their work over the course of the maker design process.

STRATEGY 4.2: CREATING METAPHORS

DURATION OF ACTIVITY: 30–45 minutes, depending on number of terms

The purpose of this strategy is to guide learners in making connections between concepts and terms they are evaluating during their research.

WHEN TO USE

The Creating Metaphors activity is valuable to use with students when they are getting familiar with new terms or concepts that relate to the maker project or design challenge. You can also use it when students need to synthesize concepts or findings or to compare groups of potential users for whom students are making their product or solution.

WHAT TO DO

STEP 1: Identify key terms, people, or concepts related to the maker challenge or design process. Arrange these terms or concepts in pairs, and provide a list of these pairs to students. When selecting terms, ask yourself, "What vocabulary from content as well as the design process will help students make connections and gain deeper understanding?"

> **ALIGNED ISTE STANDARDS FOR STUDENTS**
>
> ○ Knowledge Constructor, 3b

> **GO REMOTE**
> - Using collaborative documents or slide decks can provide ways for students to work individually and collectively.
> - With the Google Jamboard app, students can create digital sticky notes for the key characteristics and organize them according to the details.
> - Increase student creativity and independence with this activity by having students create their own informational graphics that outline the desired information using the tool of their choice.

STEP 2: Create a three-column chart. The number of rows should match the amount of details you'd like students to provide for each concept or term. (Scan the Chapter 4 Resources QR code for an example.)

STEP 3: Have students list the specific characteristics of the targeted terms in the outer columns, the left term's details in the left column and right term's in the right column.

STEP 4: Have students rewrite characteristics of the terms/people/concepts/potential users in more general language in the middle column. The purpose of this is to facilitate students in synthesizing concepts and to guide students as they make connections between related concepts.

STRATEGY 4.3: COMPARING IDEAS

DURATION OF ACTIVITY: 30–40 minutes

This strategy is a powerful way to help students connect different concepts through their similarities and differences.

WHEN TO USE

The Comparing Ideas strategy can be very helpful for introducing students to different types of concepts they are exploring and different client groups for whom they may be making. This activity

> **ALIGNED ISTE STANDARDS FOR STUDENTS**
> - Knowledge Constructor, 3b

is also powerful for supporting students as they compare their ideas to one another's and can help a group decide on what focus for their challenge they are most interested in.

WHAT TO DO

STEP 1: Divide students into small groups, then have students individually brainstorm keywords or ideas that can help them dig deeper into their topic. Suggest they create one sticky note for each idea, word, or concept that comes out of their research as it relates to their topic.

STEP 2: Ask students to share their individual brainstorm sticky notes with the rest of the group and choose two different ideas, keywords, topics, materials, or ideas to compare.

STEP 3: Give students two prompts: _____ and _____ are similar because they both _____ and _____ and _____ are different because they both _____. Ask them to outline three similarities and three differences between their ideas. Another option would be to have learners create a Venn Diagram to sort their idea (Figure 4.3). It is important that learners also can indicate their reasoning for why specific items would be similar or different.

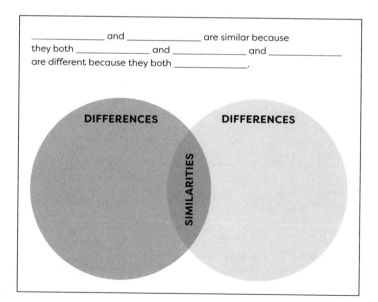

Figure 4.3 In addition to providing prompts to guide their thinking, encourage students to create a Venn Diagram to further illustrate their thinking.

> **GO REMOTE**
>
> - Any tool that allows students to identify their individual ideas, then share and rearrange them while communicating with others, is useful. For instance, while engaging in real-time videoconferencing, students could use Google Jamboard, Padlet, collaborative documents or slides, Pages, or Numbers.

STEP 4: Ask learners to collaboratively review the points they came up with for similarities and differences, then use the differences to identify specific features or details, customer needs, or materials they want to focus on.

STRATEGY 4.4: WHICH ONE DOESN'T BELONG

DURATION OF ACTIVITY: 20–30 minutes

This strategy is very useful for helping students become familiar with key vocabulary or concepts when starting a design challenge.

WHEN TO USE

The Which One Doesn't Belong strategy is best to use when students have a working knowledge of the relevant terms, and it is good to incorporate after students have done some research as it relates to the challenge but still need to expand their research.

WHAT TO DO

STEP 1: Prepare terms or phrases ahead of time that share a common link, and include one that does not belong. For best results, identify words that can be easily categorized and are the same part of speech. You could also create examples of phrases that students might find during research or details they

> **ALIGNED ISTE STANDARD FOR STUDENTS**
>
> - Computational Thinker, 5b
> - Knowledge Constructor, 3c

> **GO REMOTE**
> - Use tools that help students digitally move ideas around and show connectedness, such as MindMup, Padlet, Google Jamboard, or Explain Everything.
> - Have students use the screen-recording features of the iPad or an app such as Screencastify to talk through their explanations and groupings.

may observe when getting to know their target audience. Helping students identify examples of indicators or features of the variables they are studying can be very useful for breaking down abstract concepts.

STEP 2: Using a template such as Figure 4.4, have students identify which term or concept does not fit.

STEP 3: Have students explain why the term does not fit with the others.

LIST 1	LIST 2	LIST 3
Which item above does not belong?	Which item above does not belong?	Which item above does not belong?
Explain your reasoning:	Explain your reasoning:	Explain your reasoning:

Figure 4.4 Providing students with a graphic organizer also helps them to chunk their thinking as they work on developing and articulating their reasoning for their selections of terms that don't belong.

STRATEGY 4.5: PUZZLE STORIES

DURATION OF ACTIVITY: 30–45 minutes

This strategy is useful for helping students gain deeper understanding around key terms they are using or to jumpstart their research process. The Puzzle Stories strategy also helps students develop their visual thinking skills.

WHEN TO USE

The Puzzle Stories strategy can be used to build vocabulary students will need during the design process and help students expand their knowledge base to help them refine their research questions.

ALIGNED ISTE STANDARDS FOR STUDENTS

- Knowledge Constructor, 3c

WHAT TO DO

STEP 1: Create a list of five to ten vocabulary words. Be sure to include nouns and verbs. The words should easily combine into a story that allows students to engage in sense-making and develop deeper understanding. If the concepts are more complex, you may want to consider using fewer words. Or, you could combine words from different subject areas if you're doing a cross-disciplinary challenge.

STEP 2: Either provide photos for students or have students capture or find their own photos to represent the terms. Have students combine the photos to create their own story.

STEP 3: To bring it all together, have students review their terms and use them to create a story about the scene or object depicted in the images. Alternatively, students can construct sentences about what they see. The goal here is to provide students with voice and choice for the way they combine visuals and terminology to create a story.

GO REMOTE

- Any tool that allows students to create, mark up, and share their images and stories is valuable, such as iMovie Trailers, Clips, Explain Everything, ShowMe, Notes (for iPad or iPhone), or Google Draw.

STRATEGY 4.6: FINDING FICTION

DURATION OF ACTIVITY: 25-40 minutes

The goal of this strategy is to assist students in deepening their understanding by evaluating truths.

WHEN TO USE

The Finding Fiction strategy can assist students in researching their topic or diving deeper into a challenge.

WHAT TO DO

STEP 1: Decide if you want students to engage in this activity individually or in groups of three to five.

STEP 2: After doing some research, have each group write down two true statements and one false statement or common misconception.

STEP 3: Have one student in each group share the group's three statements.

STEP 4: Provide time for the other groups to discuss and reach consensus on which statement they believe is false.

STEP 5: Have each group share their conclusions and reasons for why the statement is false.

ALIGNED ISTE STANDARDS FOR STUDENTS

- Knowledge Constructor, 3a, 3b

GO REMOTE

- Any tool that allows students to post their ideas and have others vote on or rate them provides a highly effective way to assess the options. Powerful tools, such as Padlet, dotstorming.com, Google Jamboard, and Google Forms, are easily accessed via an online link and provide visual representations of the data collected.

STRATEGY 4.7: CARD SORT—INDUCTIVE REASONING

DURATION OF ACTIVITY: 30 minutes or more, depending on the number of cards to sort

Card sorting strategies are helpful for organizing information in a sensible way. In addition, card sorting strategies provide a way to help participants develop their understanding and evaluate connections between concepts. The big idea is to have students be able to think deeply about the terms or data sets and consider trends or patterns they see.

WHEN TO USE

The Card Sort—Inductive Reasoning strategy is best to use when students are learning key terms or data points related to the maker design challenge. This is a great activity to help students learn how to look for patterns and create relevant categories. This activity will also prepare students for looking at data that they collect later in the research element of their work.

WHAT TO DO

STEP 1: Create a list of terms or visual data; either the teacher or the student can do this. Aim for 15–25 terms for elementary learners and 20–40 terms for secondary learners. Too few terms can lead to disengagement, and too many can be too complicated. Creating ways for students to have the terms or data points on cards makes sorting easier and provides students with the opportunity to physically move ideas around.

STEP 2: Have students sort and group terms or data based on common characteristics or shared features. This activity can be done collaboratively or individually.

STEP 3: Once the terms are sorted, have students come up with descriptive titles for the groups they created.

STEP 4: Have a discussion on how students determined their groupings and the categories they came up with.

ALIGNED ISTE STANDARDS FOR STUDENTS

- Computational Thinker, 5b
- Knowledge Constructor, 3c

> **GO REMOTE**
> - Provide students with a terms list, and then have them create a Padlet wall that represents their groupings. With a digital list of terms or data sets, students can copy and paste the terms to organize them.
> - Google Jamboard allows students to collaborate and organize their ideas in real time in the same digital environment. You provide ready-made digital sticky notes with the terms or provide students with a terms list to make the sticky notes themselves.

Identifying a Target User or Audience

The most powerful design experiences are those that support learners in being able to answer the questions: What am I making? Who am I making for? Why am I making it? In order to help learners be able to identify the what, why, and who, the strategies in this section focus on developing specific skills for conducting interviews, making powerful observations, as well as collecting and visualizing data. As you review the strategies in this section, consider the focus of your maker challenge and be open to the different research methods and the authentic data students can collect and evaluate.

STRATEGY 4.8: MAKING FOR WHO

DURATION OF ACTIVITY: 30–45 minutes

The goal of this strategy is intended to help learners start thinking about the needs of a specific user who they are designing for or to define a target audience they want to focus their research on. One of the biggest contributors to false starts is that students want to jump into making and creating without thinking about who they are making for and why. This activity helps students develop an understanding around why it is important to have a specific target audience.

> **ALIGNED ISTE STANDARDS FOR STUDENTS**
> - Innovative Designer, 4b
> - Creative Communicator, 6d

WHEN TO USE

Inspired by the d.school's Wallet Project, the Making for Who activity can be useful for students starting or at the early stages of their research process. It creates an opportunity for students to think beyond their own personal experiences and dive deeper into the needs of others. (Scan the Chapter 4 Resources QR code for a link to the original Wallet Project and more resources from Stanford University's d.school.)

WHAT TO DO

STEP 1: Identify an example of a product or solution that people commonly use but that can look different or have different features based on who the intended user is. For sake of example, these steps use a wallet.

STEP 2: Ask students to describe the "perfect" incarnation of the identified product or solution, such as *Describe the perfect wallet*. Encourage students to jot down their own descriptions, whether on paper or digitally. Figure 4.5 shows an example template for this activity; you can download it from the chapter's resources.

STEP 3: Have students share their examples with a partner, and then have a whole group share-out. You can guide the conversation by showing some pictures of different wallets as examples (fanny pack, traditional leather wallet, and so on) to get participants to consider that there are many ways to meet the needs of a "wallet" and that it might look different and have different features depending on what need and user it is trying to accommodate. Ask such questions as:

○ What did you notice that was similar about people's ideas of the perfect wallet?

○ What did you notice that was different?

○ Why would it be important to identify a specific user or target audience?

GO REMOTE

○ Leverage videoconferencing tools for whole group conversations, or use breakout rooms if you choose to do this activity in small groups.

○ You also can have students use voice recording tools or voice-to-text features of tools such as Google Docs to capture initial ideas. This is especially helpful for students with limited keyboarding skills or students who like to ideate verbally.

STEP 4: Have students revise their initial description of the "perfect" wallet based on a specific user or target audience.

STEP 5: Have students evaluate how they would identify specific user needs or who could benefit from a solution they create. Some question prompts to guide this conversation include:

- How would interviewing someone be different from observing behavior?
- What other ways could you research and collect data to help you define who you are creating a solution or making something for?

PROMPT	STUDENT RESPONSE
Describe the perfect _____.	
Work in small groups to reflect on this process and jot down your thoughts on the following: • What did you notice that was similar about people's ideas of _____? • What did you notice that was different? • Show some pictures of different _____. • Why would it be important to identify a specific user or target audience?	
Making for Who? Identify an example Sample User or Target Audience you want to focus on for designing a _____.	
Draw or list ideas of how you would change your initial description based on designing a _____ for a specific user _____.	
Evaluate how you could identify specific user needs or who could benefit from a solution or design you create. Consider the following questions: • What could you learn from observing people's behavior or use of a specific object? • How would interviewing someone differ from observing behavior? • What other ways could you research and collect data to help you define who you are creating a solution or making something for?	

Figure 4.5 Prompt students to consider not only the many possible designs for a product but also how they can tailor features for specific user needs.

STRATEGY 4.9: MOM TEST

DURATION OF ACTIVITY: 20–30 minutes

The goal is to develop students' ability to ask powerful interview questions that elicit useful and substantive answers to aid their design process. In his book *The Mom Test: How to Talk to Customers & Learn If Your Business Is a Good Idea When Everyone Is Lying to You*, Rob Fitzpatrick advocates an archeological approach to interview techniques (see Step 4) and outlines key components to constructing interview questions that help interviewers uncover people's true actions and beliefs (2013). His work stems from the idea that successful questions can gather accurate information from interviewees who may not want to answer questions honestly—like a mom that answers with supportive half-truths or what she thinks you want to hear to be "helpful."

WHEN TO USE

The Mom Test strategy is very useful for helping students prepare to conduct their own interview and observations in order to identify empathetic connections and client or target audience needs.

WHAT TO DO

STEP 1: Share a video that exemplifies the Mom Test, such as The Mom Test at **youtu.be/Hla1jzhan78**.

STEP 2: While they're watching the video, have students complete a visible thinking activity to identify:

- Three main points about the Mom Test
- Two "I wonder" questions
- One connection about how strategies from the Mom Test can help identify specific needs people have (or, have them make one prediction based on the video)

ALIGNED ISTE STANDARDS FOR STUDENTS

- Knowledge Constructor, 3a, 3d

STEP 3: Have students share their answers.

STEP 4: Close the conversation by revisiting the key elements that the Mom Test uses to explore user or target audience needs:

- Explore people's life experiences.
- Dig into specifics about the past.
- Keep it short, aiming to ask three questions.
- Don't pitch your idea or possible solutions. Keep it specific to people's past behaviors and experiences.
- Aim for a time goal of 5-15 minutes for an interview.

Encourage students to consider how they could apply these principles in their own work.

GO REMOTE

- Have a whole group conversation using videoconferencing, a learning management system or workflow tool, or a discussion board to engage students in the content and share their thoughts.
- Use **wheelofnames.com** as a way of selecting students or groups of students to share out. In order to avoid "cold calling," require all students to jot down an initial response and/or confer with a peer prior to calling on individuals. In addition, instead of putting student names in the Wheel of Names, you could also put in questions you'd like students to consider or respond to. Spin the wheel, and have students explore and respond to the question you land on.
- Use **edpuzzle.com** to create and embed your questions and visible thinking prompts into the video The Mom Test. This will allow you to keep track of student participation and thinking while watching the assigned video. This can be used to help students view and analyze sample interviews or to watch an overview of the Mom Test.

STRATEGY 4.10: CRAFTING QUESTIONS

DURATION OF ACTIVITY: 30–45 minutes

This strategy is useful for helping students craft interview questions or evaluate the difference between closed interview questions, which can be answered in a word or two, and open questions, which require an elaborative answer. It is important to facilitate students in crafting powerful, open questions to make the most of the interview and data collection process.

WHEN TO USE

The Crafting Questions strategy is best used before students need to outline essential questions they want to focus on when conducting research.

WHAT TO DO

STEP 1: Provide an overview description of closed and open questions (Figure 4.6, downloadable from the chapter's resources page).

STEP 2: Provide students with sample questions to evaluate.

STEP 3: Have students identify and categorize which questions they think are closed and which ones are open.

ALIGNED ISTE STANDARDS FOR STUDENTS

- Knowledge Constructor, 3b, 3c

GO REMOTE

- Tools such as Padlet, Google Jamboard sticky notes, dotstorming.com, and collaborative documents or slides allow participants to share, view, and sort ideas. Being able to move and categorize individual questions into different categories increases interactivity as well as provides opportunities for thoughtful discussion.

CHAPTER 4: SCAFFOLDING THE STUDENT DESIGN PROCESS

Closed Questions:	**Open Questions:**
Answered with few words	Answer needs with explanation and elaboration
Good for seeing quantities	Broad
• How many days a week do you…	Answer includes details:
• How many hours or minutes do you…	• What are your reasons…
• What is…	• What is most important…
• How much of the…	• How can we…
• How many…	• Why are you…
Yes or no questions	
Multiple-choice questions	
Sample Closed Questions:	**Sample Open Questions:**
Would you recommend our product/service?	What were the main reasons you chose our product/service?
Would you consider using our product/service again?	What would make you use our product/service again?
Did you experience good customer service?	How did you feel about our customer service?
Did you like our product/service?	What is the most important feature of our product/service for you?
Are you interested in buying a product/service today?	Why are you looking for a product/service today?
Are you happy with your experience with us?	How would you describe your experience with us?
Did you find what you were looking for today?	How can we help you find what you are looking for today?

Adapted from Fio Dossetto, Open-ended questions vs. close-ended questions: Examples and how to survey users. hotjar.com/blog/open-ended-questions

Figure 4.6 Understanding the difference between closed and open questions is vital for successful interviews.

STEP 4: Ask students to consider their maker challenge and identify at least two closed and three open-ended questions that would be helpful to explore to gain more information on their topic or challenge.

STEP 5: Encourage students to share their open-ended research questions by putting them where others can view them.

STEP 6: Have students jot down one new idea they got from viewing peer questions.

STRATEGY 4.11: HEAR IT, SEE IT, QUOTE IT, CODE IT!

DURATION OF ACTIVITY: 30–45 minutes depending on the number of data points being analyzed

IDENTIFYING A TARGET USER OR AUDIENCE

Helping students develop the skills of naturalistic observation and interview data analysis, this strategy requires learners to take a deeper look at the data they are collecting from their specific research method, identify or code the type of data it represents, and then interpret and make a connection to inform future solution storming.

> **ALIGNED ISTE STANDARDS FOR STUDENTS**
> - Innovative Designer, 4d
> - Knowledge Constructor, 3b

WHEN TO USE

The best time to use the Hear It, See It, Quote It, Code It! strategy is after students have collected data from interviews, observations, or other research methods. However, be sure to introduce the Quote It, Code It! graphic organizer to students prior to conducting their research so they can use it to inform the questions they develop or their strategies for observing. (Scan the Chapter 4 Resources QR code for a digital copy.)

WHAT TO DO

STEP 1: Have students jot down quotes from interviews they collected or descriptive notes from observations in the left column of the Quote It, Code It! graphic organizer (Figure 4.7).

QUOTE IT, CODE IT! ANALYZING AND CODING YOUR INTERVIEW DATA			
Quote It! Jot down quotes from interviews	**Code It** Indicate which code best describes the type of quote from the interview.	**Meaning or Interpretation**	**Empathetic Connection**
	Interview: Past Experience New Need Questions Other:		

Figure 4.7 The Quote It, Code It! graphic organizer (excerpt shown here) can help students understand how quotes and data from an interview can exemplify a specific design goal they may want to focus on. (You can download the full template from the chapter's resources.)

> ### GO REMOTE
>
> - Encourage students to create forms with Google Forms to conduct interviews and review the data they collect in the spreadsheet as well as using the visual graphs and charts they may have access to.
> - Use cameras and audio recording tools, such as SoundTrap or GarageBand, to capture and review interviews. To increase accessibility, encourage students to use transcription tools to help them as they revisit audio interviews they have conducted. Google Meet and Zoom also offer closed captioning, which is helpful for assisting all students in revisiting interview recordings.
> - The Pages and Numbers applications support the use of multimodal exchange of ideas, offering options to create text, imagery, and audio content. This can be helpful for allowing students more modalities and options for curating, analyzing, and reflecting on the data they have collected.

STEP 2: Explain to students the different ways to categorize participant interview responses or observations they make. Discuss ways that specific quotes or descriptions can exemplify a specific element they may want to focus on. For example, data points reflect demographic trends or common themes.

STEP 3: For each specific data point, have students interpret the meaning of the quote.

STEP 4: Encourage students to identify an empathetic connection to how the data could inform their next steps in solving the problems or making solutions.

STRATEGY 4.12: VISUAL THINKING

DURATION OF ACTIVITY: 45 minutes

The goal of this strategy is to sharpen observation skills and students' ability to form empathetic connections. Observation and inference are particularly important skills for makers to develop. In addition, it is important for students to develop empathic connections to the topics they are studying and problem-solving for.

WHEN TO USE

The Visual Thinking strategy is powerful to use as students are engaging in research and either identifying or observing a specific target user or audience.

ALIGNED ISTE STANDARDS FOR STUDENTS

- Innovative Designer, 4d
- Knowledge Constructor, 3b

WHAT TO DO

STEP 1: Provide students with specific images that relate to the challenge they are studying.

STEP 2: Pose questions that foster observation:

- What's going on in the images?
- What do you see that makes you say that?
- What more can you find based on what you see?

STEP 3: Have students connect with a peer and compare responses to the images. To prompt student discussion, try such questions as:

- What can you conclude?
- What evidence supports that conclusion?
- What is your opinion of _____?
- What is the most interesting part?
- What is the purpose of _____?
- Compare two parts of the _____.

STEP 4: Engage in a whole-group share-out.

STEP 5: Have students compare and contrast their original observation with their peers' perspectives.

STEP 6: Have students evaluate why it is important to consider someone else's perspective or experience.

CHAPTER 4: SCAFFOLDING THE STUDENT DESIGN PROCESS

GO REMOTE

Because this activity focuses on observation and comparison of different perspectives, using tools that allow students to author their own work and then see the work of others is valuable. For example:

- Using Google Slides create a slide deck that includes photos or videos as well as slides where students can post their thinking and see their peers' posts. Having slides assigned to specific students can keep things more easily organized than using a collaborative text document.
- Using Google Jamboard allows students to view an image and then stop and jot down their ideas on the board. Create multiple boards if you want all students to see different images.

STRATEGY 4.13: TAKEN BY SURPRISE

DURATION OF ACTIVITY: 30–60 minutes

This activity is powerful for grabbing students' attention and sparking inquiry. This activity focuses on having students experience or observe something firsthand that sparks wonder. It also can be used to form empathetic connections.

WHEN TO USE

The Taken by Surprise strategy is powerful to use when either kicking off the topic for a design challenge or teaching a specific skill builder. For example, if you are looking to develop students' computational thinking skills, demonstrate the outcome of a specific skill or technique in a way that sparks inquiry and interest.

WHAT TO DO

STEP 1: Identify an event that would cause wonder or surprise and that you could use to teach a specific concept. For example, if you are a social studies teacher and you are going to teach about breaking social norms, break one

ALIGNED ISTE STANDARDS FOR STUDENTS

- Innovative Designer, 4d
- Knowledge Constructor, 3b

> **GO REMOTE**
>
> Any tools that help students experience an event collectively and then be able to confer to decipher its impact or cause are valuable. Try:
>
> - Collaborative documents (Google Docs or Pages) or collaborative slide decks (Google Slides or Keynote) where all teams can share their work on each slide for others to see.
> - Google Jamboard to have students post their group summaries.

and capture student reactions. If you teach science, conduct an experiment for students to observe that has an unexpected result. Or if STEM is your area, get a robot to do something interesting or make something that sparks wonder.

If you aren't comfortable doing this, you can also find a video to help demonstrate or capture students' attention. For example, PBS Frontline's documentary *A Class Divided* (1985) is about teacher Jane Elliot and the firsthand lesson in discrimination she devised for her students in 1968 (**pbs.org/wgbh/frontline/film/class-divided**).

STEP 2: Implement the event (or show a video), and focus students on an area of observation.

STEP 3: Organize students into small groups to discuss the reasons for the event as they attempt to understand it and develop questions.

STEP 4: Have a reporter from the group share the group's thinking and see if they can identify the cause of the event and reveal what happened.

Research and Define

Powerful design experiences guide learners to conduct research and evaluate data before they begin making prototypes. Focused on synthesizing information, identifying patterns and trends, and developing problem statements, the strategies in this section support learners as they engage in any level of research. In addition, engaging in the research process assists students in getting to know what solutions may already exist and contemplating how they may be revised. Developing a clear problem statement will also help learners focus their solution and later prototype development.

STRATEGY 4.14: CLAIMS, EVIDENCE, REASONS

DURATION OF ACTIVITY: 20-40 minutes based on how many claims students are required to make.

Whether students are conducting their own observations or interviews or they are engaging in more traditional research, it is important for them to be able to make a claim, support it with evidence, and explain why it is significant. This activity provides scaffolding to support students as they identify key observations, make claims, and then provide evidence and reasoning for the claims they are making.

ALIGNED ISTE STANDARDS FOR STUDENTS

- Knowledge Constructor, 3b, 3c
- Creative Communicator, 6c

WHEN TO USE

The Claims, Evidence, Reasons strategy is most useful to implement after students have gathered informational sources or have data they collected to work with.

WHAT TO DO

STEP 1: Provide students with an informational source, ask them to identify their own resources, or have them dig into data they may have collected from interviews or observations.

STEP 2: Ask students to identify three claims or takeaways based on their informational source.

GO REMOTE

- Allowing students to choose a tool they are already familiar with lets them focus on their data and analysis without the distraction of learning a new, specialized tool.
- Screencasting tools, such as ShowMe, Explain Everything, the iPad's Screen Recording feature, or Screencastify, enable students to talk through images or specific pieces of evidence, capturing their thinking aloud.

STEP 3: Have students identify specific evidence to support their claims.

STEP 4: Ask students to reflect on the reasons that their evidence supports their claims.

STRATEGY 4.15: HEAR, THINK, WONDER

DURATION OF ACTIVITY: 25–35 minutes

The purpose of this strategy is to coach learners to take in information through various senses and to engage them in higher-order thinking.

WHEN TO USE

Best used when students are analyzing data, the Hear, Think, Wonder strategy can be useful for when students are reviewing responses from interviews or observations.

ALIGNED ISTE STANDARDS FOR STUDENTS

- Knowledge Constructor, 3b, 3c
- Creative Communicator, 6c

WHAT TO DO

STEP 1: Ensure that students have an informational or data source to review, and provide a graphic organizer similar to Figure 4.8. The key to this activity is making student thinking visible and audible.

STEP 2: Ask students to identify specific things they read, see, or hear and to communicate what those things make them think. Then have students share a new wonderment.

STEP 3: Have students repeat the process using another source and write what they think and connect it to a new understanding.

I hear....	And that makes me think...	Now I wonder...
I read....	And I think...	So, now I understand....

Figure 4.8 Contemplating information they receive through various senses helps students engage in higher-order thinking.

> **GO REMOTE**
> - Provide students with the choice to create a video and share their thinking, following the template in Figure 4.8. Flipgrid is a great way for students to capture their thinking and share it with others.
> - SoundTap and GarageBand are useful tools for students to create audio samples of their thinking and wonderments.
> - Padlet and the Google Jamboard also provide opportunities for students to share their thinking and use Figure 4.8's sentence stems in creative ways.

STRATEGY 4.16: OVERHEARD QUOTES

DURATION OF ACTIVITY: 30–45 minutes

The purpose of this strategy is to encourage students to dig deeper into a quote and make inferences about a larger text or informational source.

WHEN TO USE

Overheard Quotes is a powerful strategy to help students dig deeper into their research, and also explore different perspectives of an event or phenomena. Specifically, this strategy provides a powerful way to guide student analysis when they are working on finding reliable sources, unpacking responses from interviews and observations, as well as forming empathetic connections.

WHAT TO DO

STEP 1: Generate a list of quotes about a topic, and give each student a different quote with a different viewpoint on the same theme.

STEP 2: Direct students to read their quote and write down their initial thoughts about it. You could also allow students to create a visual representation of their initial thoughts.

> **ALIGNED ISTE STANDARDS FOR STUDENTS**
> - Knowledge Constructor, 3b

RESEARCH AND DEFINE

> **GO REMOTE**
>
> To assist students in sharing their initial quotes with peers:
>
> - Create one slide for each quote with Google Slides, and assign a slide number/quote to each student. Or, put the quotes in a document and have students type their quote on their slide.
> - Allow students to put their quote on Padlet or Google Jamboard. One wall or board per quote is best.

STEP 3: Ask students to exchange quotes with another student but not discuss them. Repeat this step four more times.

STEP 4: After they exchange quotes with five peers, have students discuss the following questions in small groups or consider them individually:

- What common ideas are in the quotes?
- What conclusions can you draw?
- What questions do you have now?

STRATEGY 4.17: QUESTIONS AND COMPARISONS

DURATION OF ACTIVITY: 30 minutes

This strategy provides a structured way for learners to interact with their peers, compare findings, and make connections across informational sources or data points.

WHEN TO USE

When students are in the middle of their research process, the Questions and Comparisons activity provides them with time to reflect on their research and evaluate the findings of others. It also can be helpful for preparing for the next phase during which students will construct a specific problem statement.

> **ALIGNED ISTE STANDARDS FOR STUDENTS**
>
> - Knowledge Constructor, 3b, 3c
> - Creative Communicator, 6c

> **GO REMOTE**
>
> Some tools that can support documenting and sharing student thinking include:
> - Collaborative documents that can be shared
> - Videoconferencing tools that allow students to share their screens and talk through the details of their research with a peer
> - Videoconferencing tools that support breakout rooms for small-group work and discussions

WHAT TO DO

STEP 1: Provide students with, or have students state, a question to investigate.

STEP 2: Instruct students to use an information source or several to jot down important points from their research.

STEP 3: Direct students to interact with a peer to discuss their findings from the research. Encourage students to identify any contradictions or confusing points.

STEP 4: Have students state how their thinking has changed or developed after engaging with their informational source and their peers.

STEP 5: Have students write a claim that they can support with evidence from their research.

STRATEGY 4.18: ASSESSING CREDIBILITY JIGSAW

DURATION OF ACTIVITY: 45–60 minutes

This strategy leverages a collaborative approach to help students evaluate the credibility of a source.

WHEN TO USE

A powerful teaching tool, the Assessing Credibility Jigsaw strategy is best to use at the beginning of the research process because it focuses on helping students determine the difference between informational sources, as well as boosting their collaboration skills.

WHAT TO DO

STEP 1: Identify an informational source for students to engage with, and select three or more questions for students to consider, such as:

- Does the author or speaker accomplish the objective in the piece to effectively address the point at issue?
- Is information logical, relevant, and well supported?
- Does the author reach appropriate conclusions based on reasoning? Are their interpretations accurate?
- Are the underlying assumptions logical?
- What other perspectives on the issue should you consider?
- What other ways could you examine this information?

STEP 2: Assign a specific question to each group, and ask them to record evidence as they review the source, jotting down details, conclusions, questions, and wonderments they have based on the question they are exploring.

STEP 3: Now that all groups have reviewed the source with a specific question in mind, remix the students into groups that have a representative for each question they focused on. For example, if you have four key questions and each group considers a specific question, members of the group that considers question 1 are all number 1s, the question 2 group are all 2s, and so on. Then, when the groups are remixed, they should form new groups that have members from each of the initial focus groups, 1, 2, 3, and 4.

STEP 4: Have students join a new group comprised of representatives from all the other expert groups.

STEP 5: Working in their new groups, direct students to discuss their findings and jot down key points they hear from others in their new group.

STEP 7: Have students return to their expert groups and share what they learned. Based on what is shared and what they themselves had concluded, have students work in their expert groups to summarize their final conclusions about the credibility of the source.

ALIGNED ISTE STANDARDS FOR STUDENTS

- Digital Citizen, 2c
- Knowledge Constructor, 3b

> ## GO REMOTE
>
> It is important for students to be able to interact with their peers to compare findings and make connections during this activity. Some ways to support these steps include:
>
> - Create a template in a collaborative document that allows students to take notes when they are working in their expert groups and comparing and sharing findings with their remixed groups.
> - Encourage the use of videoconferencing screen-sharing features to increase the different ways students can share and perceive the information others are reviewing with their peers.

Defining Problems and Ideating Solutions

Just as it is important to define a problem, it is also important to carefully evaluate possible solutions. The strategies in this section guide learners through generating and assessing different ideas. Incorporating strategies that encourage learners to stay on point to meet the need of a specific target user or audience is also useful for helping increase the efficiency and relevance of the maker and design process.

STRATEGY 4.19: WRITING PROBLEM STATEMENTS

DURATION OF ACTIVITY: 15–25 minutes

The most important questions for makers to be able to answer include: What am I making? Who am I making for? Why am I making? Teaching students how to write a clear problem statement that outlines each of these questions will increase students' authentic problem-solving capabilities. This strategy will help guide students as they construct problem statements.

WHEN TO USE

The Writing Problem Statements strategy is specifically useful during the middle or end of the initial research process. Providing learners with the opportunity to construct their own specific problem statements helps them to later develop more relevant solutions, hone next steps, and focus on a specific user or audience.

ALIGNED ISTE STANDARDS FOR STUDENTS

- Empowered Learner, 1c
- Knowledge Constructor, 3b

WHAT TO DO

STEP 1: Direct students to identify a specific user or target audience you want to focus on.

STEP 2: Have students identify a specific need or problem that this group faces.

STEP 3: Ask students to identify why this user will benefit by a solution of this need or problem, then put all the pieces together into a problem statement using a frame such as:

_____ needs a way to _____ so that they can or
(user) (need)
because _____.
(reason/why)

OPTIONAL: Consider having students complete Steps 1–3 individually first if they are working in small groups, and then share their ideas with group members. This will provide more students the opportunity to become more familiar with the various ways a problem statement may develop, allowing students to explore different options for users, needs, and reasoning.

GO REMOTE

Any process that allows students to identify and evaluate the potential user, need, and reason for the need is valuable. The following tools can support this process:

- Google Jamboard sticky notes allow students to brainstorm possible users and needs per note as they discuss their reasoning.
- Videoconferencing tools that have whiteboard features offer options for students to illustrate their thinking.
- Padlet enables students to share their final problem statements and comment on those of their peers.

STRATEGY 4.20: AFFINITY DIAGRAM: CLUSTER AND RATE SOLUTIONS

DURATION OF ACTIVITY: 45–60 minutes

The affinity process is often used to group ideas after brainstorming. Once ideas are generated, participants can identify categories or themes that emerge. Then, they can use these categories to sort and display information in a way that also visualizes the data. For example, students can brainstorm problem statements, sharing one idea per sticky note. After generating ideas, they can come up with certain categories or themes that the various ideas can fall into. Each sticky note can then be placed in its respective category. The sticky notes will form a bar graph of sorts, which can be helpful for visualizing patterns.

WHEN TO USE

The Affinity Diagram: Cluster and Rate Solutions strategy is helpful to use during the solution ideation phase of the design process because it allows students to be flexible in their thinking and review workable solutions through different lenses or themes. The strategy is best when students are working together to develop or refine a problem statement or when students have developed different sample problem statements and want to work on refining the final problem statement. You could also adapt this strategy (and its companion graphic organizer, available on the chapter resources page) to use when students are brainstorming solutions or specific features of solutions they are developing.

ALIGNED ISTE STANDARDS FOR STUDENTS

- Empowered Learner, 1c

WHAT TO DO

STEP 1: Have students individually construct a problem statement (see Strategy 4.19), identify a user, a need, and a rationale. Provide a frame to help students construct their problem statement, such as _____ needs a way to _____ so that/because _____. Challenge students to come up with four to five ideas per person.

Or, if students aren't ready to have a problem statement yet, first have them individually identify potential users, needs, and reasons, writing each on a separate card, note, or space. Using these, have them then develop a problem statement.

STEP 2: Have students post their statements on a card or sticky note for other group members to see.

STEP 3: Have students work in their groups to discuss the problem statement ideas and categorize them based on similarities. Encourage students to create a vertical bar graph with their sticky notes or cards.

STEP 4: Instruct students to come up with category names for the groupings.

STEP 5: Ask each group to present their category ideas to the class as a whole. Give students three dots (blue, red, yellow, or some other variation) that they can use to vote on the problem statements, with a blue dot denoting the best statement, a red the second best, and a yellow the third best.

STEP 6: Have groups review the votes and work together as a design team to develop their final problem statement.

GO REMOTE

- Any tool that allows students to post their ideas and have others vote on or rate them is useful. For example, students could use Padlet, Google Jamboard, Google Forms, and many videoconferencing whiteboard tools to share their categories and gather their information.
- If students have sticky notes at home, they can also use the Post-it App to take photos and collaborate with others to view and move ideas around on a shared board. This app also allows users to export their Post-it Notes as image files. This can be useful if students want to share their ideas on a collaborative app like Google Jamboard or Padlet.

STRATEGY 4.21: STATE AND RANK POSSIBLE SOLUTIONS

DURATION OF ACTIVITY: 30–45 minutes

The goal of this strategy is to provide learners with a process for developing and evaluating possible solutions to the problem they are investigating and solving.

WHEN TO USE

The State and Rank Possible Solutions strategy is best to use when students are working on developing key characteristics of their solution, but before they engage in the sketching or making of a prototype. This activity can be done individually or collaboratively.

WHAT TO DO

STEP 1: Direct students to identify key elements, details, or components they think should be incorporated in their solution (Figure 4.9).

ALIGNED ISTE STANDARDS FOR STUDENTS

- Empowered Learner, 1c
- Global Collaborator, 7b

Design Team Members: or Individual Maker:		
Step 1: Identify details, elements, or components you think would be a valuable part of your solution.		
Solution Element 1:	Solution Element 2:	Solution Element 3:
Summary or value it provides:	Summary or value it provides:	Summary or value it provides:

Figure 4.9 A graphic organizer such as this (excerpt shown here) can help students clarify their thoughts while identifying and ranking elements of their design solutions. (You can download the full template from the chapter's resources.)

GO REMOTE

To provide students with ways to connect in real time, brainstorm ideas, and then share out a final summary, try any of the following tools:

- Videoconferencing tools with breakout rooms to support small-group work, such as Google Meet, Zoom, or Webex.
- Collaborative documents, such as Google Docs or Google Slides.

STEP 2: Have students write a summary for each detail or concept.

STEP 3: Ask students to rank the elements they identified in order from most important to least important.

STEP 4: Instruct students to explain the reasoning for the ranking.

STEP 5: Encourage students to determine which elements are most important and identify the best summary statement.

STEP 6: Have students or groups of students review and exchange their ideas.

STRATEGY 4.22: CONSENSOGRAM

DURATION OF ACTIVITY: 25–45 minutes

This strategy provides students with the opportunity to generate ideas and evaluate them in a visual way.

WHEN TO USE

Providing students with a visual representation of their assessment of their solution when compared against specific criteria, the Consensogram strategy is best used while students are evaluating the type of solution they want to create.

ALIGNED ISTE STANDARDS FOR STUDENTS

- Empowered Learner, 1c
- Global Collaborator, 7b

> ### GO REMOTE
>
> - Try tools such as Google Draw, Google Slides, Keynote, and Pages that provide options to use graphics and shapes to indicate individual votes or ratings.
> - Use tools that allow students to post and move ideas around simultaneously, such as Google Jamboard or whiteboard tools included with videoconferencing solutions, to help increase virtual participation.
> - Create a form with Google Forms where students rank their solution based on the criteria provided.
> - Engage students in virtual dot voting using Dotstorming.com. Participants can receive a link to the voting board, which can be password protected if desired. In addition, as manager of the board, you can choose to enable or disable the chat and commenting, as well as moderate participant anonymity.

WHAT TO DO

STEP 1: Remind students that the purpose of this activity is to help them consider the quality of their solutions. Ask them to review the rating scale of "Absolutely, Mostly, Somewhat, and Not at All," as well as the success criteria they need to meet, such as:

- Criteria 1: The solution is geared toward a specific audience.
- Criteria 2: The solution meets a specific need people have.
- Criteria 3: The solution is too similar to something that already exists.

STEP 2: Have each member of the design team rate the solution against the criteria outlined. (Scan the Chapter 4 Resources QR code for a graphic organizer that students can use.) It may be helpful to provide students with a table that at the top has the criteria listed in each column and the possible solutions one per row. Then students can place check marks to indicate if the proposed solution meets each of the criteria.

STEP 3: Ask students to review their responses and ratings and look for trends, answering the prompts:

- What did you notice in the ratings?
- What patterns are noticeable?
- What surprises you?
- What conclusions might you draw?

STEP 4: Direct students to discuss with the members of their design group how they might modify their solutions based on the information from the ratings for how well the proposed solution meets the success criteria. It can also be helpful to have students construct a short summary of their conclusions from the above reflection prompts.

STRATEGY 4.23: SOLUTION STORMING

DURATION OF ACTIVITY: 20–30 minutes

The goal of this strategy is to help learners generate and evaluate a variety of solutions or features of a possible prototype.

WHEN TO USE

The best time to use the Solution Storming strategy is when students have defined their problems and are ready to generate and evaluate ideas for possible solutions.

WHAT TO DO

STEP 1: Direct students to brainstorm as many possible solutions for their problem statements or features for their prototype as they can, but to come up with at least five ideas—even radical ones. Students can write or sketch their ideas. A graphic organizer such as Figure 4.10 can help.

ALIGNED ISTE STANDARDS FOR STUDENTS

- Global Collaborator, 7c
- Innovative Designer, 4a

Problem Statement:		
Possible Solution or Features **We will create** _____ **that** *supports/helps/* ***addresses*** _____. (can be sketched or written)	**Level of Importance**	**Create Success Criteria** What would need to take place to support or create a successful solution?
	1------------------------5 Low High	
	1------------------------5 Low High	
	1------------------------5 Low High	
	1------------------------5 Low High	

Figure 4.10 While brainstorming solutions and features, students can be practical or radical with their ideas. The ranking step will help them sort out the ideas' relative importance.

STEP 2: For each idea, have students rank how important they think it is for solving the specific problem they identified in their problem statement.

STEP 3: Ask students to indicate what they would need to do or modify in order to make their solution more viable.

GO REMOTE

To help students focus on generating possible solutions or features, provide students the option to sketch their thoughts using such tools as:

- Notes (for iPad or iPhone), which enables students to sketch and save their sketches as images
- Google Jamboard's Draw feature
- Screenshot capabilities on their smartphone or mobile device
- Paper and Padlet, which allows students to draw on paper, take photos of their sketches, and upload images to a space where they can collectively evaluate and sort

STRATEGY 4.24: SWOT ANALYSIS

DURATION OF ACTIVITY: 45–60 minutes

Commonly used in business settings, the SWOT Analysis strategy is a powerful way to evaluate possible solutions, ideas, or objectives. SWOT stands for Strengths, Opportunities, Weaknesses, and Threats or Risks (Gray, Brown, & Macanufo, 2010). The strategy provides a process for developing a desired end state while focusing on what can be improved. In addition, the collaborative nature of this activity helps students develop effective communication skills.

WHEN TO USE

SWOT Analysis is a valuable activity for students to try just before they settle on a solution and begin sketching what their prototype would look like.

WHAT TO DO

STEP 1: Have students identify their solution or a specific outcome they want to achieve.

STEP 2: Ask students to identify potential strengths, opportunities, weaknesses, and threats or risks associated with their idea or solution.

STEP 3: Direct students to summarize new conclusions they have come up with about their objective or solution.

ALIGNED ISTE STANDARDS FOR STUDENTS

- Innovative Designer, 4b
- Global Collaborator, 7c

GO REMOTE

- Using tools that allow students to collaborate and make their thinking visible is valuable for this activity. Using collaborative slide decks, such as Google Slides, to provide a specific place or slide for each group to conduct their SWOT increases productivity while working in remote, blended, or virtual settings.

Sketching

Sketching is a powerful mechanism that leads to more refined prototypes, whether in school makerspaces or industrial manufacturing. Before they make prototypes, engage students in sketching their prototype concept and creating a plan that explains how the prototype will work. Requiring learners to sketch and plan before building not only helps refine their ideas, but it is also an effective way to prevent students from wasting time and materials. You can use the strategies in this section to help students organize their thinking and their sketches, as well as engage in deeper reflection and peer feedback.

ADDITIONAL SUPPORTS FOR PEER FEEDBACK

Many of the strategies in this section involve peer feedback. To create norms that foster an effective and supportive peer feedback process, be sure to:

- Model the peer review process for students to make sure they understand the success criteria.
- Stress that feedback should be helpful and kind.
- Ensure that students understand the value of constructive feedback.
- Allow text and audio feedback.
- Allow students to revise their work.
- Have students submit a peer critiquing form with their final assignment and highlight changes they made.

STRATEGY 4.25: SKETCHING CHECKLIST

DURATION OF ACTIVITY: Throughout the sketching phase, ongoing

This strategy provides students with scaffolding support during the sketching process to increase the quality of prototyping sketches.

WHEN TO USE

The best practice is to introduce the Sketching Checklist to students before they start sketching. They can use the checklist during sketching as well to facilitate self-reflection and progress monitoring.

> **ALIGNED ISTE STANDARDS FOR STUDENTS**
> - Innovative Designer, 4a
> - Creative Communicator, 6a

WHAT TO DO

STEP 1: Review criteria with students about what they can do to successfully sketch their prototype, highlight features, and use their sketches to help explain how their prototype will work (Figure 4.11). Provide a checklist of statements to confirm, such as:

- I drew what I saw.
- I included as much information as possible.
- I zoomed to highlight something unusual/detailed/unique.
- I added labels to give more detail about color, texture, and so on.
- I wrote some "I wonder" questions about my sketch.

Figure 4.11 Provide students with sample success criteria for reflection on their sketching process. This tool can also be used to help students consider powerful elements for prototype sketching as well as to review their work for completeness.

Sketching Checklist: Did I do the Following?

☐	Draw what I **see**
☐	Included as much information as possible
☐	Zoomed to highlight something unusual/ detailed/ unique
☐	I added labels to give more detail about color, texture, etc.
☐	I wrote some "I wonder questions" about my sketch
☐	I added Color (when appropriate)
☐	I added a title and date to my sketch.
☐	I used sketching and words to record as much information about my drawing as I could.

I shared my sketch with _____ for feedback

Notes from their feedback:

CHAPTER 4: SCAFFOLDING THE STUDENT DESIGN PROCESS

> ### GO REMOTE
> ○ Using the checklist in a collaborative document (such as with Google Docs), creating an assignment or form (such as with Google Forms) out of the checklist, or providing a prompt for students to create a screencast talking through their sketch are powerful ways to use the sketching checklist in a virtual or remote environment.

○ I added color (when appropriate).

○ I added a title and date to my sketch.

○ I used sketching and words to record as much information about my drawing as I could.

STEP 2: Request that students share their sketch with a peer and jot down notes about their feedback. (See Strategy 4.26 for scaffolding related to providing formative feedback.)

STRATEGY 4.26: EVALUATING THE DESIGNER'S REASONING

DURATION OF ACTIVITY: 20–40 minutes

The purpose of this strategy is to guide learners as they analyze peer prototypes. It is important to understand the purpose and intent of design in order to provide formative feedback. This strategy provides learners with the scaffolding they need to organize their thinking.

WHEN TO USE

The Evaluating the Designer's Reasoning activity is best to use when students have completed a draft sketch of their prototype and are ready to receive feedback. This strategy provides great follow-up steps to Strategy 4.25.

ALIGNED ISTE STANDARDS FOR STUDENTS

○ Computational Thinker, 5c

○ Creative Communicator, 6d

WHAT TO DO:

STEP 1: Have students work in groups or pairs to review another team or maker's sketch of their prototype.

STEP 2: Have students use the graphic organizer shown in Figure 4.12 to collect their thoughts when reviewing another maker or design team's sketch.

STEP 3: Engage students in a large-group discussion to summarize the feedback they received and share what modifications they will make to their sketch.

Group Members:	
Product or Solution Name:	
Maker's Claim:	_____ will _____ for _____

Review the sketch to consider whether it demonstrates features of the prototype and how it will work to meet the needs outlined above.

Tell Something You Like
- I really like the way you...
- I enjoyed...

Ask a Question
- I am wondering...
- Why did you....
- I'm a little confused about....

Give a Suggestion
- Can you write, sketch, or develop a little more...
- Do you need help with...
- Maybe you can come up with a better way to...
- How do you feel about adding...

Is the sketch convincing?
Why or why not?

Figure 4.12 A graphic organizer can help students collect their thoughts and scaffold constructive peer review skills.

Figure 4.13 Use Google Forms to create a form with which students can provide feedback to their peers.

GO REMOTE

- Use tools such as Padlet that enable students to post an image of their sketch and then allow peers to add their feedback under it. Specific use of comments as well as columns is helpful.
- Create a class Google Site or location in your learning management system where students can post their sketches, and then using the content presented in the graphic organizer, create a form with Google Forms (Figure 4.13) that students can use to review maker claims and sketches as well as provide descriptive feedback.

STRATEGY 4.27: QUESTIONING AND PEER REVIEW

DURATION OF ACTIVITY: 20–30 minutes

Providing opportunities for students to develop robust, detailed sketches of how their prototype solutions will increase the efficiency of making the prototype. To make the most of the sketching phase, this strategy provides specific methods for engaging students in peer review to deliver descriptive feedback.

WHEN TO USE

The Questioning and Peer Review activity is best to use when students have completed a draft sketch of their prototype and are ready to receive feedback.

WHAT TO DO

STEP 1: Have students review another student's sketch. Encourage students to analyze the sketch for specific features of the prototype and any details that explain how the prototype will work.

STEP 2: Have students use the following question stems to create interesting questions they would ask the creator of the sketch:

- Why...?
- What are the reasons...?
- What if...?
- What if we knew...?
- What would change if...?
- What is the purpose of...?
- How would it be different if...?
- Suppose that...

STEP 3: Share these questions with the illustrator of the sketch, and have them review the brainstormed list to identify the three questions that seem most interesting.

STEP 4: Ask the illustrator to identify one or more questions to discuss with their design team.

STEP 5: Have students reflect on and share what new ideas they have about their sketches and their prototypes that they didn't have before.

ALIGNED ISTE STANDARDS FOR STUDENTS

- Computational Thinker, 5c
- Creative Communicator, 6d

> **GO REMOTE**
> - Using tools such as Google Jamboard and other digital whiteboards, students can post an image of their sketch and peers can add their feedback. Be sure to provide a variety of ways for students to pose questions and for illustrators to review them. For example, in addition to written comments, students can create video or audio clips.

STRATEGY 4.28: ACCOUNTABLE TALK STEMS FOR ANALYSIS

DURATION OF ACTIVITY: 15–30 minutes

The accountable talk stems and questions provided in this strategy guide student thinking and increase confidence, leading to richer peer feedback and analysis conversations.

WHEN TO USE

Whether students are reviewing sketches or evaluating possible problems to solve or solutions to make, the Accountable Talk Stems for Analysis strategy will help students communicate.

WHAT TO DO

STEP 1: Identify what students will be analyzing or critiquing.

STEP 2: Review the success criteria with students so they are familiar with what "good" looks like. Also review the purpose of peer feedback to provide helpful, kind, and constructive feedback to progress the work forward.

STEP 3: Provide students with accountable talk stems to choose from as they review and discuss the content they are analyzing (Figure 4.14).

> **ALIGNED ISTE STANDARDS FOR STUDENTS**
> - Empowered Learner, 1a
> - Digital Citizen, 2b
> - Creative Communicator, 6b, 6d

> **GO REMOTE**
>
> ○ No matter where students are engaged in learning, having a printed copy or easily accessible digital version of the talk stems and question starts is highly valuable.

ACCOUNTABLE TALK STEMS AND QUESTIONS FOR ANALYSIS	
Expansion • Tell me more about that. • What do you mean by _____? • How could/would you _____? • Help me understand _____.	**Perspectives** • Is there only one viewpoint on that? • Why might someone say that? • Why might someone think that? • What do you think influences their thinking or behavior?
Interpretation • Tell me more about that. What words might you use to describe _____? • _____ makes me think… • _____ makes me feel…	**Clarification** • So, you're saying _____ • Do you mean _____? • How did you interpret that?

Figure 4.14 Providing talk stems and questions like these will help deepen student thinking and guide constructive feedback.

Prototyping

Providing opportunities to engage leaners in metacognition (thinking about their own thinking) during prototyping is highly valuable. The strategies provided in this section range from providing sample student prototyping checklists to activities to help students get to know their makerspaces to resources for making. In addition, you will find strategies and sentence stems to guide students in the process of refining their prototypes at the later stages of development.

STRATEGY 4.29: PROTOTYPING PROCESS CHECKLIST

DURATION OF ACTIVITY: 10–20 minutes

By providing learners with a prototyping process checklist, this strategy increases their metacognition and improves self-progress monitoring. Using a checklist encourages students to consider what work they have done thus far and plan what they will need to do next.

> **ALIGNED ISTE STANDARDS FOR STUDENTS**
> ○ Innovative Designer, 4c

WHEN TO USE

Sharing the Prototyping Process Checklist with students prior to making prototypes is a great way to kick off the making process.

WHAT TO DO

STEP 1: Review the prototyping process checklist (Figure 4.15) with students, and explain how it will be used as the work progresses. Whether students are making physical or digital prototypes, it is important that they take the time to review and reflect on the prototyping process checklist. Be sure to support ways to make student thinking more visible during this process.

STEP 2: Ask students if they have any questions.

STEP 3: Discuss any specific elements of the checklist you think students may struggle with.

> ### GO REMOTE
>
> ○ Have students take photos or create visuals that relate to various phases of the prototyping process. For each phase, ask students to reflect on their work and provide descriptive evidence to support their claims. Students can then curate these images and reflections in a slide deck or website. Using Google Slides, Keynote, or Microsoft PowerPoint can be very helpful.
>
> ○ Have students curate prototyping portfolios that include visual representations of individual phases of the prototyping checklist, then create accompanying reflections based on their progress and demonstration of the criteria for that phase. Using Google Sites is a way to make this a highly collaborative and reflective experience for group prototyping.
>
> ○ Have students construct video reflections or screencasts where they share visualizations of their prototypes and talk through specific features. Some tools that can be helpful include Clips, Screencastify, or WeVideo.

PROTOTYPING PROCESS CHECKLIST

PHASE 1: UNDERSTANDING THE PROBLEM
○ I learned more about the problem.
○ I know who I am making this for.
○ I know how to explain the problem to others.
○ I need to meet with my teacher.

PHASE 2: BRAINSTORMING
○ I sketched or created a visualization of my ideas to solve the problem.
○ I learned more about ways to solve the problem.
○ I worked with others to get more ideas.
○ I made a final sketch or visualization of my new learning.
○ I learned from others and combined those ideas with my own.
○ I need to meet with my teacher.

PHASE 3: CREATING A PLAN TO TEST PROTOTYPES
○ I have a plan to test whether my prototype works.
○ I know what I need to learn more about.
○ I am organizing my information.
○ I made a chart or graph to understand my information.
○ I know what works and what doesn't.
○ I need to meet with a teacher.

PHASE 4: MAKE A PROTOTYPE
○ I am building the prototype using my design.
○ I am taking pictures/video and writing down changes to my design.
○ I need to meet with my teacher.

continues

Figure 4.15 Providing a checklist like this early in the making process will help students self-monitor and stay focused.

PROTOTYPING PROCESS CHECKLIST continued

PHASE 5: TEST A PROTOTYPE
- ○ I tested the prototype from my plan.
- ○ I used the right tools or process to test my prototype.
- ○ I documented the results of my test (data).
- ○ I organized the data to make sense of it.
- ○ I analyzed my data and identified key findings.
- ○ I took pictures/video or wrote down what was happening.
- ○ I need to meet with my teacher.

PHASE 6: EVALUATE THE SOLUTION
- ○ I used the data to decide if it worked.
- ○ I learned from others and may have changed my design.
- ○ I made changes to my prototype based on what I learned.
- ○ I need to meet with my teacher.

PHASE 7: LAUNCH YOUR SOLUTION
- ○ I can write or say directions so someone else can use my prototype.
- ○ I am making a video to show how my prototype/solution works.
- ○ I am making a step-by-step storyboard to show how my prototype/solution works.
- ○ I am presenting to an audience to explain how my prototype/solution works.
- ○ I need to meet with my teacher or peer reviewer.

PHASE 8: REFLECT ON YOUR SOLUTION
- ○ I am getting feedback from people other than in my classroom.
- ○ I thought about what went well.
- ○ I thought about what could have been better.
- ○ I know what I would do differently next time.
- ○ I know what step was best for me/my team.
- ○ I shared my prototype/solution and explained my thoughts/ideas.
- ○ I need to meet with my teacher.

STRATEGY 4.30: MAKERSPACE WALKABOUT

DURATION OF ACTIVITY: 15–20 minutes

This strategy helps learners be strategic about the resources they use.

WHEN TO USE

Prior to having students jump in and make prototypes, give them a chance to get to know your makerspace. The Makerspace Walkabout strategy is an important step to help learners evaluate the resources for making that are available to them and to review guidelines and expectations. Be sure to remind students to review their sketch prior to doing this activity to gather ideas about what they might need.

WHAT TO DO

STEP 1: Have students assess their readiness to start making prototypes.

STEP 2: Have students take a walk around the makerspace and survey the available resources. To expand options for accessibility, provide learners with opportunities to also explore virtual tools for maker learning. Encourage students to consider how they might use specific features of the tools. For example, students can identify questions they may have and assess how they may want to use the tool.

STEP 3: Ask students to identify which resources they will need or want to use. This step is important so that students limit waste and maximize the resources they have access to.

STEP 4: Ask students to discuss steps they can take to ensure safety when working in the makerspace or with its unique tools and capacities. As always in addition to writing, provide students with options to share their thinking in a variety of multimodal formats.

ALIGNED ISTE STANDARDS FOR STUDENTS

- Innovative Designer, 4b, 4c

> **GO REMOTE**
>
> - This activity can be modified to accommodate a digital makerspace as well as to help students use commonly found materials at home that are useful for rapid prototyping. Cardboard is an extremely valuable resource for at-home maker learning. Be sure to include parents in this activity or conversation too.

STRATEGY 4.31: PROTOTYPING ACCOUNTABLE TALK STEMS

DURATION OF ACTIVITY: 15–30 minutes

Accountable talk stems and questions for prototyping guide student thinking and increase confidence, leading to richer peer feedback and analysis conversations about prototyping iteration.

WHEN TO USE

The Prototyping Accountable Talk Stems will support students as they self-reflect and provide feedback while peer reviewing prototypes.

> **ALIGNED ISTE STANDARDS FOR STUDENTS**
>
> - Innovative Designer, 4b, 4c

WHAT TO DO

STEP 1: Review the accountable talk stems (Figure 4.16) and how they can be used for reflecting and self-assessing, or peer review and feedback.

STEP 2: Outline and communicate the most appropriate method for students to share their peer feedback or to submit a self-reflection.

> **GO REMOTE**
>
> - Provide ways for students to demonstrate and explain their prototypes in real time or video. Tools that help students collect and exchange peer feedback include Flipgrid, Padlet, Google Jamboard, and Google Forms.

Observation/Conclusions	Testing
• My test shows _____ because _____. • I think my results are _____ because _____. • I see...	• What I think is working well with my prototype is... • I think _____ helps _____. • What I think is working well is _____. • According to my observations _____. • I know _____ because _____. • I'm using _____ to collect my data. • I wonder if I modify...
Clarification	Extension
• What problem does your prototype solve? • Explain more, please... • What is your evidence? • What do you think your findings mean?	• I wonder... • I would like to add _____ to improve my prototype or design. • Next time you might want to test _____.
Confusion	Notes:
• I don't understand _____. • I'm confused about _____. • I'm wondering _____.	

Figure 4.16 Scaffolding peer feedback with talk stems can lead to deeper analysis and conversations about prototyping iteration.

STRATEGY 4.32: SCAMPER

DURATION OF ACTIVITY: 30–60 minutes

Standing for Substitute, Combine, Adapt, Modify/Magnify, Put to other uses, Eliminate/Minify, Rearrange/Reverse, SCAMPER is a brainstorming technique that helps students consider alternative ideas (Gray, Brown, & Macanufo, 2010).

WHEN TO USE

The SCAMPER strategy is especially useful for helping students either work collaboratively or individually on evaluating and revising their prototypes.

ALIGNED ISTE STANDARDS FOR STUDENTS

○ Innovative Designer, 4b, 4c

WHAT TO DO

STEP 1: Have students work in groups to review each other's prototypes and explanations for how their prototype works and what it represents.

STEP 2: Instruct students to use the SCAMPER accountable talk stems (Figure 4.17) and to consider adaptations and feedback they can provide to the prototype design team or maker.

SCAMPER ACCOUNTABLE TALK STEMS

SUBSTITUTE
- _____ could also use _____.
- Another feature to add could be _____.
- Instead of _____ you could use _____.
- Another opportunity is to _____.

COMBINE
- What if you connected _____ to _____?
- What if you added features from _____.
- _____ could use this too.
- You could join this with _____.

ADAPT
- I think you could alter _____.
- What if you modified _____?
- A new purpose for your solution/product could be _____.
- What if you used _____ instead of _____?

MODIFY/MAGNIFY
- _____ could be larger.
- Your prototype could be more effective if you make _____ smaller.
- Your prototype could be more effective if you make _____ larger.
- What if you zoom in on _____ for your sketch?

Figure 4.17 Provide students with talk stems to support the SCAMPER brainstorming technique.

GO REMOTE

- Providing ways for students to demonstrate and explain their prototypes in real time or video is very helpful. Give students options for collecting and exchanging peer feedback in various forms, including collaborative documents; posts on Flipgrid, Padlet, or Google Jamboard; forms made with Google Forms; or annotated photos.

- What if you use color to _____?
- What if you change the direction to _____?
- What if you use _____ material instead?

PUT TO OTHER USES
- Your solution reminds me of _____.
- I wonder if your solution could also be used for _____?
- A new way to use this is to _____.
- In an emergency someone could use this to _____.

ELIMINATE/MINIFY
- What if you removed _____?
- Could you take _____ away?
- What if you minimize _____?
- What if you made _____ smaller?
- What if you had less _____?

REARRANGE/REVERSE
- What if you put _____ before _____?
- What if you change your layout to _____?
- What if you did the opposite of _____?
- What if you put _____ after _____?

STEP 3: Direct students to complete the graphic organizer for providing feedback using the SCAMPER criteria (Figure 4.18).

STEP 4: Direct the design team to review the feedback and summarize what modifications they will make to their prototype.

SCAMPER *ACTIVITY FOR PROTOTYPE DEVELOPMENT* **DESIGN TEAM/ MAKER NAME:** _____ **REVIEWER TEAM:** _____		
CRITERIA	**QUESTIONS TO CONSIDER**	**NEW IDEAS**
Substitute	Who else could use your product or solution? What feature or detail might you add?	
Combine	How could you connect, join together, merge, or blend aspects or pieces of your prototype or solution?	
Adapt	What could you gain from altering, updating, or adding to your prototype or solution?	
Modify/Magnify	How might you change the color, size, material, fabric, direction, length, or feature size?	
Put to Other Uses	Can you find an unusual way to use or a new place to use your solution or prototype?	
Eliminate/Minify	If you removed or took pieces away, how would your solution change? Would it be better or weaker?	
Rearrange/Reverse	What would happen if you changed the order, layout, direction, or pattern in your solution or prototype?	
After reviewing the above feedback, what changes will you make to refine your prototype? Explain why you are choosing to make these modifications.		

Figure 4.18 When combined with the talk stems in Figure 4.17, a graphic organizer like this can help students process and apply peer feedback to improve their prototypes.

Evaluation

Learning is social in nature. Providing opportunities for students to connect with their peers as well as authentic audiences adds a powerful dynamic to any maker learning experience. The strategies within this section provide methods that not only heighten cognitive engagement in the iterative process but also can be modified to meet any learner where they are at.

STRATEGY 4.33: SIX THINKING HATS: LAUNCHING YOUR WORK

DURATION OF ACTIVITY: 30–60 minutes

Developed by Edward de Bobo in 1985, the Six Thinking Hats strategy helps students work in groups more effectively. Six specific roles, which are symbolized by six colored hats, are assigned to students in a group. Each student in the group provides a unique viewpoint and perspective based on the color thinking hat they were assigned. The six hats and their roles are Blue/Leader, White/Thinking, Red/Feeling, Green/Creativity, Black/Cautious, and Yellow/Positivity. While students aren't literally wearing hats, the hats and colors represent different perspectives and opportunities for development. It can be helpful to provide participants with color-coded cards to help them focus on the different perspectives. If you have design teams smaller than six, combine specific areas of focus.

WHEN TO USE

Although you can use this activity during various stages of the design process, it is a fun and creative way to help students assess how they would launch their solution or share it with a larger audience.

WHAT TO DO

STEP 1: Have students generate ways that they could raise awareness or launch their solution to its intended user. Encourage students to be creative.

ALIGNED ISTE STANDARDS FOR STUDENTS

- Global Collaborator, 7c

GO REMOTE

- Use videoconferencing tools with breakout rooms and leverage tools that support how students are able to jot their ideas down in the moment to increase student productivity. Shared collaborative documents, shared whiteboard tools, and screen-sharing features are all helpful.
- Have students create a short presentation to demonstrate the thinking from each perspective and final idea for launching their work to support students' workflow as they present to the larger group.

STEP 2: Assign each group member a specific role or "hat to wear," and review the questions they should consider in that role as the group discusses the ideas generated in Step 1 (Figure 4.19).

STEP 3: Encourage students to be creative and stick to their roles. Have the Blue hat facilitate the small-group discussion, the White hat share first followed by the Red, Green, Black, and Yellow hats. After all students have spoken, the Blue hat can invite others to add more to the discussion. The purpose of this activity is to have as many perspectives as possible to refine the overall idea.

STEP 4: After engaging in the discussion, have students summarize their final idea for launching their solution and reflect on the process of using the Six Hats strategy to improve their thinking about the topic. Some questions to consider include:

- How did analyzing the topic through the lens of the six hats improve your thinking about the topic?
- How did your thinking about the topic change?
- What new ideas emerged and were refined through this process so that you could create?

EVALUATION

HAT	ROLE PURPOSE	QUESTIONS TO ANSWER
Leader: Blue Hat	• Process control • Focus • Big picture • Agenda • Summary • Time management	• What thinking is needed? • What have we done so far? • What do we need to do next?
Thinking: White Hat	• Information • Figures • Facts • Data	• What are the facts? • What information do we have? • What information do we need?
Feeling: Red Hat	• Fear • Impact on others • Feelings • Intuition	• How does this make me feel? • What do I like about the idea? • What don't I like about this?
Creativity: Green Hat	• Creative thinking • Alternative solutions • Refine • Develop ideas	• What new ideas are possible? • What is my suggestion? • Can I create something new? • Is there an alternative plan?
Cautious: Black Hat	• Risks • Potential problems • Obstacles • Downsides • Weaknesses	• What is wrong with this? • Will this work? • Is it safe?
Positivity: Yellow Hat	• Best scenario • Benefits • Positive thinking • Optimism	• What are the good points? • Why does this work? • What are the strengths? • How will this help us?

Summarize your final idea for launching your solution to its intended user:

Reflection: Reflect on the process of using the Six Hats strategy to improve your thinking about the topic. Some questions to consider include:
- How did analyzing the topic through the lens of the six hats improve your thinking about the topic?
- How did your thinking about the topic change?
- What new ideas emerged and were refined through this process so that you could create?

Figure 4.19 The Six Hats strategy helps students focus their ideas while still considering multiple perspectives.

STRATEGY 4.34: THINKING CUBE

DURATION OF ACTIVITY: 20-45 minutes

The Thinking Cube activity guides students as they reflect on the feedback process.

WHEN TO USE

The Thinking Cube is a powerful way to engage students in peer feedback at various stages of the maker process. You can use this tool to assist students as they reflect on the design and maker process.

WHAT TO DO

STEP 1: Explain the six types of thinking the cube faces represent (Figure 4.20):

- Describe: Provide attributes, details, or characteristics of the design process.
- Compare & Contrast: Identify similarities and differences of their ideas to ones that already exist.
- Associate: Make connections to how they can use the design process and skills in the future.
- Analyze: Identify different perspectives they encountered during maker learning.
- Apply: Explain how to use their solution.
- Argue for or Against: Identify advantages and disadvantages.

STEP 2: Prepare enough cube templates for students to use individually or share. Have students assemble the cubes. If using paper, they will need tape.

STEP 3: Assign students to groups of three or four.

STEP 4: Have all students turn their cube to the Describe side first. Starting with the Describe side provides a way to ground the group in the most basic details of the work.

> **ALIGNED ISTE STANDARDS FOR STUDENTS**
> - Global Collaborator, 7c

STEP 5: Have group members take turns rolling the cube and deciding what they will discuss or reflect on.

STEP 6: Conclude the activity with reflection questions, such as:

- Which prompt was the least difficult?
- Which was the most difficult?
- Which was the most enjoyable?
- Which prompt was the most beneficial for learning new information?
- How has your knowledge of the topics increased?

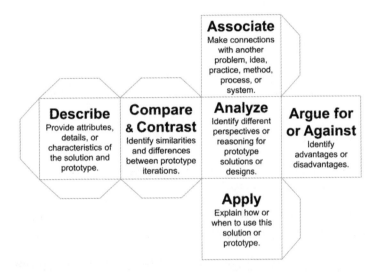

Figure 4.20 Useful at many stages of the maker process, the Thinking Cube activity combines a craft, a game, and reflection prompts.

GO REMOTE

- The fun of this activity is to do it in real time. Engaging students in whole-class or small-group discussion using the cubes is best. Encourage students to post their response in shared spaces such as Padlet, in a collaborative spreadsheet from Numbers or Google Sheets, or using Google Jamboard sticky notes.

STRATEGY 4.35: METHODS FOR SHARING STUDENT WORK WITH AN AUTHENTIC AUDIENCE

DURATION OF ACTIVITY: Varied; depending on whom the final products are being shared with, this process can range from one class period to an ongoing period of sharing curated students' work in an online environment for a specific audience to view.

These methods provide guidelines and mechanisms for celebrating and sharing student products and work with an authentic audience or can be used to support the process of sharing authentic work in order to receive feedback from an audience outside of their peers or classmates.

WHEN TO USE

It is best to engage with an authentic audience toward the end of the design process or to support the iterative feedback and revision process.

WHAT TO DO

STEP 1: Provide your audience with questions they can ask you or sentence stems to help them learn more.

STEP 2: Provide a presentation or use a graphic organizer or infographic to highlight features about your product and design process.

STEP 3: Leverage physical and digital tools to share projects and celebrate the design process! For example, Resource 3.16, Student Portfolios, provides a great starting point for developing student portfolios that can also be used to launch student work to an authentic audience. In addition, Strategy 4.29, Prototyping Process Checklist, and reflection-based strategies, such as 4.28, 4.31, 4.33, can also be used to outline and guide the student portfolio or launch process development.

ALIGNED ISTE STANDARDS FOR STUDENTS

- Creative Communicator, 6d

> ## GO REMOTE
>
> - Try website creation tools, such as Google Sites, Weebly, or Smore, to curate the process of the work and include a variety of digital reflections of specific phases of the process, feedback gathered, and iterations made.
> - Have a live (in-person or virtual) showcase where students present their work and people can ask questions, using Google Meet, Zoom, or YouTube.
> - Have students create videos about their process and product and share those with an authentic audience, using iMovie, WeVideo, or Da Vinci.
> - Have students create infographics that explain the process and product and sharing with an intended audience, using Canva or Adobe Spark.

Next Steps

Chapter 4 Resources

- Break the design process down into specific steps, and identify strategies that will provide students with support and scaffolding before and during their design process.
- Consider which digital tools and platforms students could use to document the specific stages of the design process.
- Assess accountable talk and question methods and sentence starters to shape feedback and collaboration experiences.
- Focus on developing specific student skills for various parts of the design maker process.
- Scan the Chapter 4 Resources QR code to check out useful links, templates, and resources for this chapter.

Reflection

After reading Chapter 4, take some time to consider how its ideas apply within your context using the questions below.

- What type of supports and scaffolding do my students benefit from the most?
- How can I guide students at various parts of the design thinking process to visualize and document their work and their thinking?
- What local groups or organizations exist that students can share their authentic work with?

Expand Your Reach and Launch Maker Learning for All

By the end of this chapter, you will:

- Evaluate the importance of starting with the why when introducing maker learning within your school system.

- Identify ways to leverage Maker Champion teams to model inclusive maker learning practices.

- Gain strategies you can use to engage adult learners in developing an inclusive maker learning mindset.

View from the Field: Invest the Time

WARNING: Just because you have a team of Maker Champions does not mean that everyone else will adopt inclusive maker learning practices. School leaders also need to invest in building teacher capacity in the areas of inclusive maker learning. Those who do will see higher rates of inclusion and integration of maker learning in their districts.

In working with a variety of school systems, I have met school leaders who take a very intentional, phased approach, dedicating time for teachers to dive in, make powerful connections, and develop next steps to support maker learning for all students. Others I have worked with believe that teachers learn by observing their peers in informal settings and will use makerspaces and resources when they see fit.

Each of these types of leaders has a strong rationale for their actions. I have found, however, that the leaders who take the time to invest in building educators' understanding around the value of maker learning, who address how to make it accessible to all students, and who identify what resources are necessary have higher educator engagement and commitment to this work. Educators in their systems are more likely to make meaningful connections between standards, curriculum, and the process of authentic problem-solving and making. School systems that provide the time to coach administrators and teachers through a series of intentional professional learning opportunities move ahead of their counterparts at an accelerated rate.

Build Understanding Across Stakeholder Groups

Creating an inclusive maker learning culture does not start with furnishing a makerspace, purchasing 3D printers, or collecting cardboard. Instead, it begins with a school system's ability to define and communicate their core values and beliefs around inclusion, accessibility, and innovation. To have maximum effect, these communications must reach all stakeholders: district leaders, school administration, teaching faculty, students, and families.

Simon Sinek, in *Find Your Why* (2017), purports that innovative leaders inspire change by starting with the why behind their work. Sinek warns that many organizations start with what they do, then how they do it, and neglect communicating *why* they do it. Starting with the why, moving to the how, and then to the what provides opportunities for inspiration and innovation to develop in steadfast ways.

Following Sinek's reasoning, a powerful definition of maker learning offers a jumping-off point for stakeholders to investigate what key elements increase the accessibility of maker learning experiences and resources. Then your work should focus on developing a strong rationale for why an inclusive maker culture is advantageous and necessary. Once this is in place, the focus of professional learning should turn toward developing a deeper understanding of the Universal Design for Learning (UDL) Guidelines and what applying these principles in the context of maker learning experiences looks like. (Chapters 3 and 4 offer activities and ideas to assist stakeholders in visualizing this.)

To inspire change at a systemic level, you need to unpack inclusive maker learning, addressing such essential questions as:

- Why is it important to develop an inclusive maker learning culture?
- How do we use Universal Design for Learning Guidelines in the context of maker learning?
- What do makerspaces, design studios, and their resources offer students?

Specifically, school leaders and educators should focus on what it looks like to increase accessibility within learning experiences and environments. Start with what people are most familiar with and provide concrete examples of what makes that learning environment highly accessible and inclusive. One option may be to provide participants with some common examples of how learner variability is addressed within a learning environment or lesson, such as offering students a specific choice of tools and methods they can use to demonstrate and express learning. Another set of examples could model how information is presented to students in a way to help them perceive it and act strategically, such as bolding specific terms or directive words within a student task or using graphic organizers to construct meaning.

After providing examples to get started, expand this work by having participants elaborate or generate more examples, relating them to aspects of the design process and elaborating on what can improve these learning experiences and environments. Sometimes, it is interesting to develop sample scenarios, environments, or student needs and have participants consider what elements can be redesigned or changed in a way that would increase inclusiveness for all. To gain more ideas, check out the easy-to-use and adaptable activities and resources in Inclusive: A Microsoft Design Toolkit.

HOW-TO STRATEGIES:
Spread the Word

Designed to build deeper understanding and inspire action, the strategies in this chapter focus on helping team members gain a deep understanding of the larger call to action around creating an inclusive maker culture. Taking a strategic approach with all stakeholders provides consistency in how maker and design resources are perceived and used.

STRATEGY 5.1: MAKER LEARNING AND UDL CARD SORT

DURATION OF ACTIVITY: 25–40 minutes

RECOMMENDED NUMBER OF PEOPLE: 1 or more

WHAT YOU'LL NEED:

- Cards with examples or scenarios of UDL-inspired maker learning experiences and uses of the makerspaces (Scan the Chapter 5 Resources QR code for sample cards.)

- Answer key for sort (Scan the QR code for an example.)

The purpose of card sorting is to provide educators with examples of the UDL principles of Representation, Engagement, Action, and Expression within the maker learning process and while using a makerspace or its resources. This activity is a powerful way to familiarize participants with the vocabulary of the UDL Guidelines. The learning takes place when educators engage in dialogue and must evaluate which description or example fits into which UDL principle. Sample cards with descriptions of what the UDL Guidelines and checkpoints look like in action during maker learning are provided. Aim for 30–100 example cards; too few is too simple, too many is overwhelming.

WHEN TO USE

The Maker Learning and UDL Card Sort activity is best to try when participants have already engaged in foundational learning about what inclusive maker learning is and why accessibility with this type of learning is valuable. It is also helpful for participants to already have an awareness of the UDL Guidelines, so consider providing a copy of the Guidelines to reference while they engage in the card sort activity. Encourage participants to engage in dialogue about why they believe each of the cards fits with a specific principle. I've found it helpful to encourage participants to look for key terms in the scenarios that relate to the overarching UDL principles.

ALIGNED ISTE STANDARDS FOR EDUCATORS

- Collaborator, 4a
- Learner, 1a

GO REMOTE

It may seem tricky to engage participants in this very physical activity in a virtual environment. To help facilitate this activity in a virtual environment, the following tools and processes provide options for allowing participants to move ideas around while evaluating connections to the UDL Guidelines.

- Create cards in Google Draw so that participants can easily sort the ideas while using a collaborative document in Google Docs or Google Slides.
- Create the categories and cards in Padlet or Google Jamboard, and allow participants to sort their ideas in the app.
- Provide participants a list of the statements that are on the cards. This can be helpful because it provides participants with more ways to perceive the details on the cards and to refresh their memories.
- Try an online tool for card sorting: The Card Sort Tool from UXtweak (**UXtweak.com/card-sort-tool**) offers the ability to record a session and allows participants to sort cards into specific categories, as well as label their own categories in open card sorts.

WHAT TO DO

STEP 1: Provide participants with the cards describing scenarios and examples (Figure 5.1). Explain the three UDL principles they will use for sorting categories.

STEP 2: Ask participants to work collaboratively in groups of three to five individuals to review each scenario or example on the cards. Then have participants evaluate which UDL principle the example or scenario fits. It is likely that some participants will see how the example could actually fit more than one principle (Representation, Engagement, Action, and Expression). This is okay. The goal is to prime educators to consider what it really can look like to design makerspaces and learning experiences that incorporate different methods for representation, engagement, action, and expression of learning.

STEP 3: Provide time for participants to self-assess their categorizations. Provide participants with an answer key that they can use to reflect on their categorization and card sorting. Remember, this isn't about having perfect responses, so reassure participants that they may see multiple category fits.

Figure 5.1 Provide each group of participants with categories to sort their cards into. Having different sets of the Card Sort cards in different colors per group can help with organization.

STRATEGY 5.2: CAMPFIRE

DURATION OF ACTIVITY: 20–30 minutes

RECOMMENDED NUMBER OF PEOPLE: Large groups

WHAT YOU'LL NEED:

- Cards with key terms or concepts that pertain to maker learning, inclusion, and makerspaces that people will have had some familiarity and experience with (Scan the chapter's QR code for samples.)
- A place where cards can be posted for all to see ahead of time, such as a wall

The goal of this activity is to allow colleagues to learn from others' past experiences through storytelling.

ALIGNED ISTE STANDARDS FOR EDUCATORS

- Leader, 2c
- Collaborator, 4c

WHEN TO USE

The Campfire strategy is a powerful way to use the experiences of Maker Champions and other early adopters to teach others. It works best with large groups, which increase the likelihood of different experiences and findings being shared. Make sure, however, that participants know that they don't have to be a seasoned maker expert to share an insightful story for others to learn from. Arrange the room in a campfire-like semicircle, and prepare a list of the terms that participants can review from their seat. You could even create a fun and relaxed atmosphere by embracing the campfire theme: Play a crackling fire video or cricket sounds in the background, encourage participants to wear flannel, and serve s'mores bars.

WHAT TO DO

STEP 1: Arrange the room in a circular or semicircle campfire-like setup.

STEP 2: Provide all participants with an individual list of terms that match the cards posted on the wall (or other space all can see). I recommend thinking about this like a T-chart: One side has all the terms on the wall, while the other side is empty.

STEP 3: Volunteers opt in, choose one card from the wall, and read it aloud. They then tell an introductory story about their experiences. Some key questions participants should consider when sharing about the selected topic include:

- What did you do?
- What went well that others should replicate?
- What would you recommend that other teachers do or not do?
- What impact did it have on students?

STEP 4: After sharing the story, participants then place the card on the opposite side of the T-chart (Figure 5.2). Have a Maker Champion kick off this activity by sharing first so that colleagues can see the process modeled and gain confidence.

Figure 5.2 Organize the room so all participants can view the list of terms at the front, and provide each participant with their own list of terms to reference. Being able to move cards from one side to another also helps participants keep track of which topics have been covered and which stories have already been told.

GO REMOTE

- This strategy works well in a whole-group videoconference setting. Use digital whiteboards to post and move the terms around or signify which ones participants choose.

STRATEGY 5.3: A DAY IN THE LIFE OF A MAKER

DURATION OF ACTIVITY: 20–30 minutes

RECOMMENDED NUMBER OF PEOPLE: 2 or more

WHAT YOU'LL NEED:

- A specific UDL-aligned strategy or resource you want participants to learn about in the context of maker learning
- Educators or learners who have experience using the target UDL-aligned strategy or support who are willing to share specific experiences

The goal of this strategy is to help participants develop their understanding about maker learning and acquire insights from the experiences of others. By pairing less experienced participants with teachers or students who have experience with integrating the UDL Guidelines into maker learning experiences or environments, you create opportunities for participants to learn from and empathize with those who already have experience with inclusion and making.

ALIGNED ISTE STANDARDS FOR EDUCATORS

- Designer, 5a
- Analyst, 7a

WHEN TO USE

The A Day in the Life of a Maker strategy is best to use when participants want to dig deeper into others' experiences with maker learning. While you can implement this strategy with a minimum of two participants, it is best to consider a wide variety of interviewees. To make the most of this strategy and build deeper understanding,

> ## GO REMOTE
> - Use whole-group videoconferencing to conduct the interview, and then have participants use breakout room features to do Steps 4–6.
> - Participants can create digital storyboards using Comic Life, Pages, Adobe Spark, or any tool that supports image or PDF annotation.

incorporate perspectives from students as well as teachers and encourage interviews to focus on a specific instructional strategy or resource.

WHAT TO DO

STEP 1: Introduce the interviewee and a specific UDL-aligned maker strategy that participants will be exploring through an interview.

STEP 2: Outline descriptive questions that can help the participants gain a deeper understanding of the use and impact of the specific UDL-aligned resource or strategy.

STEP 3: Have participants conduct the interview while jotting down their observations and key takeaways. Encourage participants to focus on all different parts of the activity, key outcomes, and interviewee reflections. To increase accessibility, record the interview via video and/or audio. Doing so will provide options for using transcription and closed captioning tools, as well as make revisiting parts of the interview easier for participants.

STEP 4: Have participants share their observations with a partner and then invite individuals to share with the whole group. To provide opportunities for learners to gain confidence and increase the chance of total participation, incorporate the Ripple Effect, which is the process of asking all participants to construct a response that they share and confer with a peer and then providing opportunities for whole group share out (Himmele & Himmele, 2017).

STEP 5: After sharing observations, pair participants to outline together the key perspectives, takeaways, and tips provided by the interviewees.

STEP 6: Ask the participant pairs to construct an artifact that captures what an ideal implementation of their specific strategy would entail. One option would be for participants to create a storyboard that illustrates what an ideal interview with a learner would look and sound like. Be sure to provide participants a choice for the medium with which they would like to demonstrate their learning. To expand participants' opportunities for personalization, suggest using digital tools for podcasting, video creation, modeling, coding, or 3D or graphic design to demonstrate understanding.

STRATEGY 5.4: FILLING IN THE GAPS

DURATION OF ACTIVITY: 30–45 minutes

RECOMMENDED NUMBER OF PEOPLE: 3 or more

WHAT YOU'LL NEED:

- A dedicated space for participants to share their ideas that other participants are able to access
- Sticky notes (paper and/or digital)

The purpose of this strategy is to produce an account of what a powerful maker learning experience entails in order to gain deeper understanding and clarity about what inclusive maker learning looks like in action, and to assist participants in understanding the value that intentional, inclusive maker learning offers.

ALIGNED ISTE STANDARDS FOR EDUCATORS

- Citizen, 3a
- Analyst, 7a

WHEN TO USE

The Filling In the Gaps strategy is best to use when you want participants to gain insights and review data related to high-impact, inclusive maker learning. Due to the collaborative nature of this activity, it is best to include as many participants and perspectives as possible. The more people you include, the more likely you are to identify potential gaps.

> **GO REMOTE**
>
> - Tools to create a digital storyboard include Comic Life, Pages, or any annotation tool that allows participants to download an image or PDF of a storyboard and annotate it. For instance, Adobe Spark is great for creating highly visual representations.
> - iMovie Trailers can offer options for adding authentic imagery and filling in key details in the subtitles of the iMovie template.
> - Clips provides an alternative way to engage in this activity. With this iOS-based app, participants can create short video clips to illustrate and visualize what they consider to be an example of high-impact maker learning.

WHAT TO DO

STEP 1: Instruct participants to create a list of insights they have about maker learning.

STEP 2: Instruct participants to repeat this process, making a list of insights or takeaways from the UDL Guidelines.

STEP 3: Ask participants to create an artifact that visualizes these key insights in action (Figure 5.3). No matter what type of product participants choose to create to communicate and visualize their key takeaways, the artifact needs to:

- Identify the key idea or concept
- Include a diagram, photo, or collage
- Provide a short description or sample dialogue of what the key concept or insight would look like in action

For example, participants could create a hand-drawn or digital storyboard. (Templates are available from Google Drive Templates.) Alternatives to traditional storyboarding include using Padlet's Timeline format or graphic design tools such as Canva.

STEP 5: Leave a blank scene box or space for the insights you would like to improve or learn more about.

STEP 6: Focus on the blank scene boxes to generate ideas.

STEP 7: Have participants share and review each other's work. Invite participants to add additional ideas.

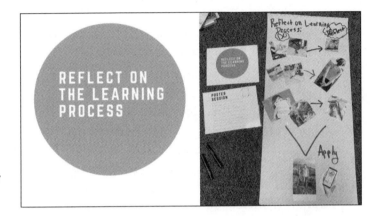

Figure 5.3 Participants can create visualizations of their key takeaways that are digital or physical.

STRATEGY 5.5: ASSUMPTION BUSTING

DURATION OF ACTIVITY: 40 minutes or more

RECOMMENDED NUMBER OF PEOPLE: 6 or more

WHAT YOU'LL NEED:

- Space to share your ideas so all can see
- Sticky notes (paper and/or digital), collaborative documents, or whiteboard tools

The intention of this strategy is to identify assumptions that stakeholders (administrators, teachers, students, parents, and so on) may have about maker learning and reject or confirm them.

ALIGNED ISTE STANDARDS FOR EDUCATORS

- Collaborator, 4d

> ### GO REMOTE
> - Gather the list of assumptions and questions in one session or prior to the session. Google Forms and survey tools are helpful for creating more flexibility. Encourage participants to contribute to and share their lists in a place that is easy for other participants to access.
> - Provide opportunities for those who listed the assumptions to listen to the reflections of other participants. One way to do this is to have Maker Champions and other relevant stakeholders create video or audio interview snippets of their responses to the assumptions or questions posed. In addition to making this easier to share, it is also a way to conduct these interviews and gather stakeholder experiences asynchronously. These interview samples can be shared during the real-time meeting, or they can be used to implement this strategy asynchronously. To facilitate capturing these interviewee/stakeholder snippets, try having participants post them to Flipgrid. Others can then watch the videos on the platform and add comments on the interview responses.

WHEN TO USE

The Assumption Busting strategy is best to use after introducing the vision of maker learning and is powerful for helping participants consider what elements do and do not fit the criteria of inclusive maker learning. Because this strategy requires participants to list assumptions they hold, the more diverse the participation group the better.

WHAT TO DO

STEP 1: Have participants work collaboratively in small groups to make a list of ten assumptions they have about maker learning.

STEP 2: Rewrite each assumption as a question.

STEP 3: Elaborate on the question with three options for possible solutions or answers.

STEP 4: Ask at least six people involved in maker learning, such as Maker Champions and their students, to share their perspectives and responses to the questions.

STEP 5: Ask all participants to compare their initial assumptions to the direct experience and perspectives shared by the Maker Champions and their students.

STEP 6: Encourage participants to summarize how this process confirmed or challenged their initial assumptions or gave them new insights.

Next Steps

- Develop strategies and opportunities to introduce inclusive maker learning to the larger school community.
- Build educator capacity and awareness around the Universal Design for Learning principles and how they can be leveraged when planning maker learning experiences.
- Highlight the inclusive vision of maker learning and provide basic entry points into the work.
- Maximize teacher and student success stories and experiences.
- Create opportunities for educators to engage in hands-on skill development in the areas of design and computational thinking.
- Formulate ways to capture and assess stakeholders' current state of understanding during the launch of inclusive maker learning. Use this data to address gaps and misconceptions or to develop professional learning offerings.
- Scan the Chapter 5 Resources QR code to check out useful links, templates, and resources for this chapter.

Chapter 5 Resources

Reflection

After reading Chapter 5, take some time to consider how its ideas apply within your context using the questions below.

- How can you work within your school system's different levels of leadership to provide introductory and skill-building experiences to a wide range of educators?

- What methods can you use to capture and make use of successful inclusive maker learning experiences and reflections that are already taking place within your school system?

- What are potential assumptions stakeholders may hold about inclusive maker learning? How might you work to anticipate and address these assumptions?

- Where might staff struggle and excel in applying the Universal Design for Learning principles?

Continuous Improvement and Assessing Program Growth

By the end of this chapter, you will:

- Gain exercises and strategies for collecting progress-monitoring data for program development.

- Explore methods for evaluating data and communicating next-step action planning stages to meet diverse stakeholder needs.

- Evaluate models for implementing ongoing personalized professional learning experiences and educator skill sets to support inclusive maker practices.

View from the Field: What's the End Game?

Creating an inclusive maker culture can be a big change for your school district, and such organizational change can be slow. I've seen so many school system leaders get to this stage of developing an inclusive maker culture and then let their focus waver. Some leaders believe the work will continue as it started without much intentional planning and progress monitoring. Others divert their efforts to focusing on maintenance and replenishing dwindled supplies in the makerspace, and still others come to a screeching halt assuming the job is in the hands of the teachers.

Now is *not* the time to drop the ball, because this stage of the work presents a tipping point. Push forward, don't slide back: Continue to gather data, identify a focus for strategic program development, and plan your next steps. Scaling back on a systems-thinking approach increases the risk for stunting the organizational growth and change that has taken place. In some instances, for example, once leaders believe that teachers have had an introduction to inclusive maker learning and the maker resources, tools, and materials are procured, the next steps of the work scales back to focus solely on what consumable resources are needed for the next school.

Obviously long-range budgeting and planning are important. School systems must continually push to evaluate, keep, drop, and add resources that continue to support the development of student and educator skills and vision of inclusive maker learning moving forward. Resource maintenance and management are not the only elements needed to create a thriving inclusive, innovative maker culture, however. Continuing to increase stakeholder buy-in and commitment is vital to its success. Leadership and stakeholder conversations that come back to "things" versus purpose-driven resource selection, instructional planning, and program development for student needs are a red flag. At this stage, school systems must leverage the larger vision and definition of inclusive maker learning to guide action step planning and identify the necessary steps for resource evaluation and ongoing capacity building, evolving the incentives for engaging in the work as the maker learning culture evolves.

Commit to Supporting Complex Change

Outlining critical components that facilitate successful organizational change, the Knoster Model for Managing Complex Change provides a valuable framework for assessing the current state of a maker learning culture, identifying needs, and planning next steps (Figure 6.1). One of the unique things about Knoster's model is that it implies that if a specific element is missing, the highest-impact change will be unlikely to take place. In other words, in order to achieve ongoing programmatic growth, essential elements must be present (Knoster, Villa, & Thousand, 2000). To inspire change and move the program forward as a whole, you need all five essential elements:

- **VISION FOR AN INCLUSIVE MAKER LEARNING CULTURE:** Create a vision statement focused on the rationale or "why" behind the move to develop an inclusive maker learning culture. This will provide a strong foundation of surface-level understanding of maker learning to build on.

- **MAKER AND DESIGN SKILLS NECESSARY FOR HIGH-IMPACT MAKER LEARNING:** Educators and learners need to develop specific skill sets to create the most dynamic, inclusive maker experiences possible. Specifically, skills related to design thinking and computational thinking can be intimidating to master. Providing opportunities for different groups of stakeholders to hone their skills also works to ease anxiety around change. The higher the confidence level educators have around their skill sets, the more likely they are to create maker learning experiences rooted in the Computational Thinker and Innovative Designer ISTE Standards for Students.

- **INCENTIVES FOR ENGAGING IN MAKER LEARNING:** School districts are notorious for having numerous goals, projects, and initiatives going on simultaneously. While these goals, projects, and initiatives are rooted in positive intent, the volume of initiatives can lead to organizational fatigue. To increase participation and garner buy-in, it is important to offer incentives for educators to take on the work of creating an inclusive maker learning culture.

- **RESOURCES FOR MAKER LEARNING:** There is nothing worse than being asked to do a job without having the right resources. Some of the powerful resources needed for creating an inclusive maker culture include time, materials, funding, coaching, capacity building, or having the right people at the table in the right seats. When resources are thin or lacking, frustration and inaction are likely to arise.

- **MULTIPHASE ACTION PLAN:** Creating a multiphased approach with ongoing progress monitoring, as well as consistent evaluation of goals and action steps, is pivotal to the long-term success of an inclusive maker culture. Failing to gather data, make adjustments, and formulate next steps can lead stakeholders to feel like the work has stalled or even in some cases digressed. Long-range action planning and progress monitoring is the key to helping move all stakeholders forward and to build momentum. In addition, having a clear action plan with specific steps and designated champions of the work can help to avoid confusion about the work.

Vision	Skills	Incentives	Resources	Action Plan	=	Success
Vision	Skills	Incentives	Resources	Missing	=	False Starts
Vision	Skills	Incentives	Missing	Action Plan	=	Frustration
Vision	Skills	Missing	Resources	Action Plan	=	Resistance
Vision	Missing	Incentives	Resources	Action Plan	=	Anxiety
Missing	Skills	Incentives	Resources	Action Plan	=	Confusion

Figure 6.1 You can use Knoster's Model for Managing Complex Change as a lens for assessing your system-wide inclusive maker learning culture and identifying areas for growth. Adapted from Teagle Foundation, n.d.

Table 6.1 provides an outline of questions to consider and steps to take when developing a high-level commitment to and competence surrounding inclusive maker learning practices.

TABLE 6.1 Action Step Planning Checklist

SUPPORTIVE ELEMENTS	QUESTIONS TO CONSIDER	SAMPLE ACTION STEPS
Vision: Create opportunities to develop a shared vision and understanding of maker learning and the UDL Guidelines, as well as the reasons they are both necessary for student achievement.	• What does inclusive learning look like in action? • What skills and literacies should learners develop through maker experiences? • How can the ISTE Standards for Students help drive this work? • Why do all students need access to maker learning experiences and resources? • If you believe they do, how do you design maker learning experiences to be as inclusive as possible?	☐ Create a shared vision and definition of inclusive maker learning. ☐ Devise a team of Maker Champions that are willing to identify, test, and evaluate specific practices and resources. ☐ Create opportunities for stakeholders to make connections to the vision and dive into assumptions.
Skills: Identify the skills and areas of expertise that educators and students will need to engage in high-impact, inclusive maker learning.	• What skills do the ISTE Innovative Designer and Computational Thinker Standards for Students outline for educators and learners? • What other ISTE Standards might you incorporate? • What knowledge or expertise do educators and learners need to access maker learning experiences and environments? • What opportunities do educators have for collaborating in planning and trying new maker experiences and inclusive practices?	☐ Outline specific activities that can be used during the design process to develop specific skills. ☐ Identify specific techniques and technologies that can be used to develop student knowledge and dispositions. ☐ Create opportunities for stakeholders to learn from each other.

continues

SUPPORTIVE ELEMENTS	QUESTIONS TO CONSIDER	SAMPLE ACTION STEPS
Incentives: Outline preexisting opportunities within your school system that coincide with the work around maker learning, accessibility, and inclusivity.	• What current incentives exist in your system for engaging in maker learning and instructional innovation? • What current methods of assessment, grading, or reporting offer avenues to measure skills and competencies that take place during maker learning? • How can existing requirements for teacher evaluation and certification support the development of an inclusive maker learning culture?	☐ Review student data and identify specific areas for growth and make connections to specific skills that can support growth in this area. ☐ Take the time to connect the dots between the ISTE Standards for Students, UDL Guidelines, maker learning, and current initiatives. ☐ Recognize teacher leadership work in ways that support the professional growth of others across your school system.
Resources: Identify the necessary resources to supply and effectively implement inclusive maker learning.	• What physical resources are needed? • What digital resources increase opportunities for student accessibility and engagement? • How will a diverse group of stakeholders be able to provide input in the process of resource selection? • How will time be allocated to the development, planning, and reflecting on this work?	☐ Foster partnerships with community organizations and businesses that can donate resources for maker learning. ☐ Research how current and emerging technology can be leveraged to increase access to maker learning experiences, resources, and spaces (physical or digital). ☐ Identify the lifespan of specific maker resources and create a long-term budgeting plan to sustain access to these resources. ☐ Provide professional learning opportunities for Maker Champions to engage in new learning. ☐ Provide time for all educators to engage in professional learning that allows them to create actionable outcomes and steps.

COMMIT TO SUPPORTING COMPLEX CHANGE

SUPPORTIVE ELEMENTS	QUESTIONS TO CONSIDER	SAMPLE ACTION STEPS
Plan: Identify specific steps worked out to direct actions toward future goals for increasing inclusion and maker learning.	• What steps are needed to move all stakeholders to future goals? • How can you create a shared process for stakeholders to understand what needs to be done and how? • Who will lead the work, provide a timescale, oversee resources, and monitor progress?	☐ Co-develop and define specific entry points for maker learning, the ISTE Standards for Students, and the UDL Guidelines within specific curricular areas. ☐ Provide educators ready-to-use UDL-aligned supports within the makerspace or maker experiences. ☐ Dedicate a leader to oversee this work from a systemic perspective. ☐ Develop a timeline that supports the gradual release of responsibility for implementation.

Surveys: Where the Model Meets the Makers

Another way you can apply Knoster's Model for Managing Complex Change to strategies and methods for evaluating an inclusive maker learning culture is through surveys. Creating surveys for stakeholders to evaluate the presence of specific elements of Knoster's model can be helpful for identifying gaps to focus on. In my district, for example, we asked educators to evaluate elements of maker learning through the lens of Knoster's model using the survey modeled on Table 6.2.

TABLE 6.2 Sample Survey for Assessing a Maker Learning Launch

ELEMENT	PROMPT	1	2	3	4
Vision	Vision of inclusive maker learning	I do not know the vision around maker learning or how it relates to our school mission and vision.	I know the vision but am not sure how to bring it about in my school/system.	I think I know what maker learning is and why it is important but am still a little skeptical.	I have a clear understanding of and can articulate our vision around maker learning and why it is important to our school mission and vision.

continues

ELEMENT	PROMPT	1	2	3	4
Skills	Instructional skills for designing inclusive maker learning experiences within the current curriculum	I do not have adequate skills to successfully implement inclusive maker learning within my curriculum.	I have minimal skills to successfully implement maker learning within my curriculum.	I have some basic skills for implementing inclusive maker learning within my curriculum but would need to develop my skills to do this consistently.	I have a variety of instructional skills and strategies to implement inclusive maker learning within my curriculum.
Incentives	Incentives for integrating maker learning experiences within current curriculum	I do not see any incentives for integrating maker learning and am not motivated to leverage maker learning to foster student innovation.	I see maker learning as a way to foster student innovation, but I do not see any incentives for adding it to my current workload.	I see the implementation of maker learning as a way to foster student innovation and am motivated to do so, but the incentives within my school system are low.	I am motivated to integrate maker learning within my learning environment to foster student innovation. My school system provides incentives that motivate me to engage in this work.
Resources	Resources (professional learning/materials/space/activities) for integrating maker learning experiences within current curriculum	I do not have access to resources (professional learning/materials/space/activities) for integrating maker learning experiences within current curriculum.	I have minimal access to resources (professional learning/materials/space/activities) for integrating maker learning experiences within current curriculum.	I have sufficient access to resources (professional learning/materials/space/activities) for integrating maker learning experiences within current curriculum.	I have ample access to resources (professional learning/materials/space/activities) for integrating maker learning experiences within current curriculum.

ELEMENT	PROMPT	1	2	3	4
Plan	Action plan for getting started with integrating maker learning experiences within the current curriculum	I do not know how I would start to integrate maker learning skills or experiences into the current curriculum, and I do not know where to get support.	I have access to some maker learning activities I can implement, but I am not sure how they support my curriculum and additional support is not available.	I can identify where to get started with maker learning within my curriculum, but there is not a lot of additional support available.	I can think of multiple entry points where I can integrate maker learning skills or experiences into the current curriculum, and there is adequate support available to help me get started or expand my work in this area.

Success Metric Checklist

In addition to the scales and success criteria provided within the sample survey, you can use the following checklist to guide the initial introduction and develop implementation steps that set the stage for successful, inclusive maker learning. This checklist can be used to signal what further data collection and analysis may be needed.

- ☐ The vision of inclusive maker learning is published, clear, easily accessed, and consistently communicated.

- ☐ Educators can connect the dots between inclusive maker learning and other initiatives.

- ☐ The skills necessary to implement inclusive maker learning are intentionally developed, and educators have access to supports for further skill development.

- ☐ A variety of incentives for integrating maker learning into the current curriculum are available and communicated for administrators as well as educators and students.

- ☐ The resources educators and learners need to successfully engage in the planning, implementation, and assessment of inclusive maker learning are readily available.

☐ There is a clear timeline and phased approach to support the gradual release of responsibility for developing necessary skills and the implementation of inclusive maker learning for all educators and students.

Use Data to Make Informed Decisions and Evaluate Professional Learning

To help you plan the next steps and help your inclusive maker culture thrive, analyze the data you collected from surveys (Table 6.2), observations, and reflections from the checklist. Use this data to identify specific areas of focus and target stakeholder groups that need development and support. In this chapter's "How-to Strategies" section, we will review specific examples of methods and materials that you can use to continue to gain insights into the specific needs of different stakeholder groups. Once you determine a specific area for development based on the data, use the following steps to help you narrow in on the specific stakeholder group (students, teachers, administrators, parents) to focus your work on using the how-to strategies. In addition, the following steps provide a powerful way to visualize and share your data and analysis.

1. Identify the most significant data points you want to focus on for developing or sustaining an inclusive maker culture, such as: Secondary teachers aren't sure how design thinking fits into their current curriculum.

2. List all of the potential stakeholders impacted or connected to this data. For example, create a wide-ranging list of specific content areas or grade levels.

3. Review your list again, and add any groups you may have missed.

4. Use the following questions to identify a specific stakeholder group to focus your work on:

    ○ Based on what you learned through the data, who will relate to this most closely or care the most?

    ○ What do they care about?

    ○ What action would you like them to take?

5. Identify potential benefits and risks. For instance, ask:
   - What are the benefits if your stakeholder acts the way that you want them to?
   - What are the risks if these stakeholders do not take action?
6. Articulate your point of view for what to focus your action steps on and which particular stakeholder group is going to be the focus. Convey what is at stake, and keep it succinct: a complete and single sentence.

You have the strategies to create an inclusive maker learning culture. How will you determine if you are successful at building the capacity of educators and impacting learning? The most innovative changes in school systems require time for adaptation, adjustment, and refinement. Therefore, we must be willing to extend support and methods for gathering evaluation information over time. To bolster your ability to evaluate the professional learning you provide, leverage the following frameworks and methods to make sense of the data you collect and determine the effectiveness of your efforts. To combat the three most common mistakes that hinder evaluating the effectiveness of professional learning (Guskey, 2003), be sure to:

- Identify desired results and success criteria for professional learning
- Diversify the elements of professional learning evaluation
- Measure the effect size of selected professional learning strategies and methods
- Use professional learning evaluation data to inform action planning for future professional learning

Identify Desired Results and Explicit Success Criteria

As you set out on your journey to create or develop an inclusive culture of maker learning, remember that this work is filled with intention, is ongoing in nature, and must be systematic. When you select strategies for engaging educators in this work, begin by outlining the desired professional learning outcomes and success criteria for achieving these outcomes. Creating success criteria will help you to determine how your goals for professional learning can be assessed as well. For example, identify a specific strategy you will implement during professional learning and consider the statement: *If educators leave this professional learning only learning/knowing/able to do _____ our program will move forward.*

Once you determine the desired outcomes, you can develop specific success criteria. Success criteria allows you to determine what professional learning outcomes look like at varying levels of success and completion. Once the success criteria are determined, you can narrow in on which methods for collecting data will be most meaningful. Figure 6.2 illustrates sample success criteria for specific professional learning strategies as well as possible methods that you could use for collecting relevant data.

SAMPLE STRATEGY	SAMPLE SUCCESS CRITERIA	POSSIBLE METHODS OF DATA COLLECTION
Strategy 2.1: Unpacking the Boxes	• Participants can justify their choices and criteria used to evaluate ideas or solutions for creating an inclusive maker learning culture. • Participants can state and identify specific challenges or areas that lack clarity. • Participants are confident in their ability to identify priorities and outline next steps in the work.	• Survey • Interview • Observation • Demonstration • Pre- and post-test of teacher knowledge and skills • Design of learning experiences produced before and after the professional learning • Pre-assessment and post-assessment data • Student data outcomes • Artifacts of students learning
Strategy 2.2: On the Cover	• Participants can demonstrate understanding of inclusive maker learning by identifying in detail what needs to be known to teach about inclusive maker learning to others with various possible points of view on it. • Participants can ask follow-up questions that focus or broaden inclusive learning. • Participants can ask follow-up questions to gain understanding of an assigned topic concerning the wants and needs of a specific audience or other stakeholders. • Participants can evaluate the advantages and disadvantages of using different mediums to present a particular topic or idea.	

Figure 6.2 Develop concrete and measurable success criteria for professional learning strategies you implement. This will help you evaluate the impact of the professional learning.

Diversify Elements of Professional Learning Evaluation

People and organizational change are complex. Evaluations of professional learning should be multidimensional (Table 6.3). Once specific and measurable success criteria are determined, you may want to consider diving deeper into evaluating additional elements of the professional learning experience. In addition to measuring the impact of professional learning strategies on the development of participants' skills and knowledge, consider participants' reactions to the professional learning experiences as well as how participants perceive their ability to implement new knowledge and skills. Incorporating measures of *self-efficacy*, the level at which someone perceives their ability to succeed in a particular situation, into the evaluation of professional learning also can help identify needed next steps as well as shed light on the likelihood of participants taking the next step and applying their new knowledge and skills in their professional practice.

TABLE 6.3 Diversify the Elements of Professional Learning Evaluation

ELEMENTS OF PROFESSIONAL LEARNING	MULTIDIMENSIONAL PROFESSIONAL LEARNING EVALUATION	
	WHAT IS MEASURED OR ASSESSED	VALUE FOR NEXT-STEP PLANNING
Participant Reactions	• Participant satisfaction • If participants saw the professional learning experience as worthwhile and time well spent	• Participant reactions can lend powerful insights to the likelihood that they will want to continue the work and encourage others to also engage in this new learning and develop their professional practice.
Participant Learning	• Participant knowledge, skills, attitudes, and beliefs	• As participants are able to see how they are gaining new skills, knowledge, and resources to be successful, they are more likely to put the time and effort into applying their new learning and gain confidence, increasing self-efficacy.
Participant Use of Knowledge and Skills	• Evidence of change in professional practice and student data	• Implementing newly gained skills provides the ability to then move the conversation to assessing the impact of this professional learning on student achievement.

Measure the Effect Size of Strategies and Methods

In short, calculating an *effect size* allows you to see the impact of your professional learning efforts on teacher and student outcomes. Calculating an effect size can help reduce the likelihood that success is random or by chance. Additionally, you can use effect size to detect a relationship or difference between the impact of one professional learning strategy or method over another. These measures of success can be pertinent and persuasive when a school system is juggling multiple projects and initiatives and the competition for funding and resources is fierce. You can gather the numbers you need to calculate an effect size between a pre-assessment and post-assessment using very basic spreadsheet functions. Create a spreadsheet with four columns: Participant Name (or Participant Number to keep it more confidential), Pre-assessment Score, Post-assessment Score, and Individual Effect Size.

After entering your data, choose five cells where you can add functions for calculating some useful statistics:

1. Calculate the average of the pre-assessment scores (use the AVERAGE function in Google Sheets or Microsoft Excel).

2. Calculate the average of the post-assessment scores.

3. Calculate the standard deviation of the pre-assessment scores (use the STDEV.S function in Google Sheets or Microsoft Excel).

4. Calculate the standard deviation of the post-assessment scores.

5. Average the standard deviations of the pre- and post-assessment scores that you calculated in steps 3 and 4.

Now, calculate the effect size by subtracting the pre-assessment average from the post-assessment average and dividing the result by the average standard deviation: (post-assessment average − pre-assessment average) / standard deviation average.

The larger the effect size, the more likely it is for the professional learning method or strategy to have an impact on the outcome. Performing an effect size calculation is most practical to use when creating a professional learning evaluation tool that provides a quantifiable score or number.

USE DATA TO MAKE INFORMED DECISIONS AND EVALUATE PROFESSIONAL LEARNING

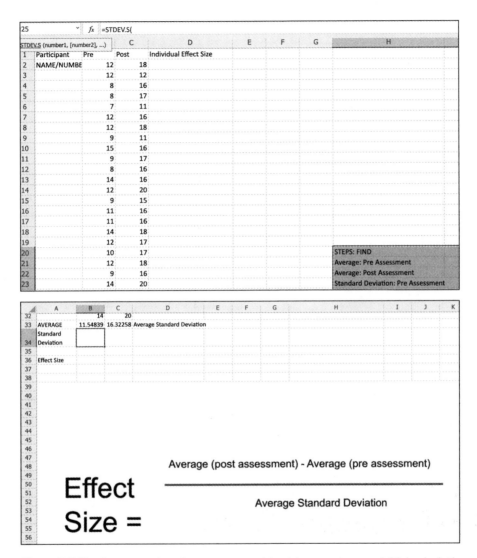

Figure 6.3 Here's one way to set up your spreadsheet to organize your initial calculations.

Use Data to Inform Action Planning

After gathering a variety of data from a variety of professional learning evaluation tools, review the data, describe what you notice and wonder, and then based on this develop a next-step goal for professional learning. To help you organize your steps, you can download the Action Plan Tracking Sheet (Figure 6.4) from the Chapter 6 Resources.

ACTION PLAN TRACKING SHEET					
GOAL:					
Professional Learning Strategy *What is the method? What will be done?*	**Method** *Specifically, how will participants engage in this professional learning?*	**Acting Party** *Who will participate?*	**Frequency** *How often will this professional learning strategy be implemented?*	**Completion Date**	**Verification Artifacts** *Which artifacts will serve as evidence that the professional learning strategy has been implemented?*

Figure 6.4 Use the Action Plan Tracking Sheet to plan which professional learning strategies may be needed next.

HOW-TO STRATEGIES:
Evaluating Programmatic Growth

In addition to using survey techniques, strategies such as an "empathy canvas" (Strategy 6.1) can provide a way for stakeholders to illustrate what messages and actions they are perceiving. Using the elements of the Knoster Model for Managing Complex Change as a lens to evaluate completed empathy canvases also provides a way to identify areas of strength and opportunities for growth. No matter which area of the model or element you want to focus on, Strategy 6.2, The What, The Who, The Do, provides a way to brainstorm, plan, and prioritize needed actions.

STRATEGY 6.1: EMPATHY CANVAS

DURATION OF ACTIVITY: 10–20 minutes

RECOMMENDED NUMBER OF PEOPLE: 3 or more

WHAT YOU'LL NEED:

- Empathy Canvas template (scan the Chapter 6 Resources QR code for a sample or search online for variations)
- Collaborative space that enables participants to review each other's work
- Sticky notes (paper and/or digital)

The purpose of this strategy is to develop a profile of what students or educators are doing, thinking, and saying about maker learning and the makerspace. Creating an empathy canvas is a powerful way to consider the different perspectives and needs that people in your organization may have. This activity can be more insightful than survey methods but relies on participants' keen observation skills. In addition, participants may need to be coached through what to look for during their observations.

ALIGNED ISTE STANDARDS FOR EDUCATORS

- Collaborator, 4a
- Learner, 2a

WHEN TO USE

Identifying a specific stakeholder persona to focus on is useful for focusing a group's attention during the Empathy Canvas activity. For example, your stated purpose could be to gain insights to the specific experiences and perceptions of educators, students, administrators, or any other valued stakeholder. The Empathy Canvas template guides participants to identify what members of specific stakeholder groups are seeing, saying, doing, feeling, hearing, and thinking. It is best to use this strategy when you are interested in diving into specific perspectives.

The more observations and variety in the specific personas being observed, the more detailed understanding of people's current needs you can gain. The Empathy Canvas

> **GO REMOTE**
>
> Participants can complete this activity prior to or during a virtual meeting. In any case, it will be important for participants to be able to view and discuss the other empathy canvases.
>
> - Create a collaborative slide deck with Google Slides, Keynote, Microsoft PowerPoint, or similar to provide images of the empathy canvases for all participants to view. Participants can then use the commenting features to exchange feedback, observations, and elaborations that come out of the collective discussion.
> - Use the image upload feature of Padlet to share empathy canvases, and then have participants post feedback on them. For example, the Reactions feature can be enabled to allow participants to note commonalities or common trends. Also, the different Padlet formats (Shelf, Timeline, Canvas) create opportunities for participants to sort the empathy canvases by common themes or connections.
> - Participants can also create their own empathy canvas in apps that support sketching, such as Google Jamboard and Notes (for iPad or iPhone). By combining Notes with the iPad's camera, participants can capture, annotate, diagram, or mark up images.

strategy is powerful for understanding how stakeholders are currently experiencing the various elements of maker learning environments and culture.

WHAT TO DO

STEP 1: Identify stakeholder groups you want to focus on and observe within the context of inclusive maker learning, such as classroom teachers, building administrators, or specific student groups.

STEP 2: Prior to participants making their observations and drawing conclusions, provide them with a specific area of focus, such as:

- The makerspace and resources
- UDL strategies to support maker learning

- Innovative Designer or Computational Thinker standards (ISTE Standards for Students)
- Crafting maker challenges
    - Making connections to curriculum
    - Assessing maker work

STEP 3: Provide a template for participants to use to record their observation (Figure 6.5), or have them draw one. Be sure the template includes the name of the stakeholder group they are focused on.

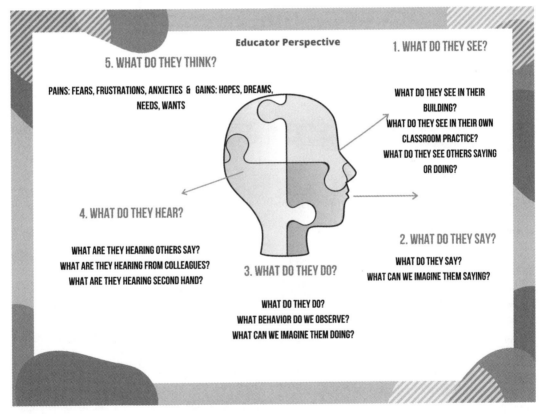

Figure 6.5 A template can help participants focus on key issues during the Empathy Canvas activity.

STEP 4: Ask participants to use a variety of their senses and keen observation skills to capture and summarize common things they hear other colleagues say, see them do, or know they are thinking about pertaining to the topic selected. Remind participants that because this isn't an interview, in addition to relying on their observation skills and senses, they will also be making some inferences at times. This strategy is about using observation skills to collect data, and then using that data to visualize and describe a specific stakeholder's point of view, thoughts, words, and so on as they pertain to a specific area of focus. Some key prompts to use are:

- What do you hear _____ saying?
- What do you think _____ sees?
- What do you think _____ hears?
- What do you think _____ is thinking about?

STEP 5: Provide time for participants to share and elaborate on their empathy canvas. Include opportunities for participants to clarify or ask questions.

STRATEGY 6.2: THE WHAT, THE WHO, THE DO

DURATION OF ACTIVITY: 25–45 minutes

RECOMMENDED NUMBER OF PEOPLE: 3 or more

WHAT YOU'LL NEED:

- Space to compile participants' ideas so all can review
- Sticky notes (paper and/or digital)

The What, The Who, The Do strategy provides a way for participants to brainstorm, plan, and prioritize needed actions. Some school systems may choose to do this activity with administration first, and then bring other stakeholders into the activity after the What component of the strategy is drafted.

ALIGNED ISTE STANDARDS FOR EDUCATORS

- Collaborator, 4a
- Leader, 2a

> ## GO REMOTE
>
> - During a virtual session, assign participants a specific board on Google Jamboard to draft their responses. Participants can then easily view other participants' responses and use the sticky note feature to add feedback. Feedback can even be color-coded by type of feedback using the various color options for sticky notes.
> - Participants can create their own graphic organizers using Google Draw, Notes (for iPad or iPhone), or other sketching apps to illustrate their ideas. Then these graphic representations can be added to a collaborative document or slide deck for collective review. Provide participants with key questions or elements they should be looking for as they review each other's work. Feedback can also be shared by adding comments or creating a two-column table: On one side list specific success criteria or elements to focus on, and use the other side to document the feedback for those elements.

WHEN TO USE

This strategy is great for diving into a specific element or stage of the work, such as identifying the need for shared vision, skills, incentives, resources, action planning, and so on. Once the focus of the work is determined, it will be easier to develop a plan of who (person or group) can act in strategic ways to move the work forward by developing action steps to address a problem. This activity can be especially useful for developing a plan for makerspace management and oversight.

The number of participants recommended for this strategy can vary. In fact, it may be most valuable to do this activity multiple times with different stakeholders as it pertains to the role they will play in the action planning process.

WHAT TO DO

STEP 1: Communicate the specific aspect of the project or element that participants will be focusing on, such as creating a shared vision, skill development, offering incentives, identifying or procuring resources, and so on.

STEP 2: Have participants work in groups of three to five to identify large goals to narrow the focus of the conversation, such as to determine who will be in charge of the makerspace and maker resource management. Giving participants the time to brainstorm around the need or area of focus will be beneficial.

STEP 3: Construct a two-column matrix. Label the first column "Do," and the second "Who." (Scan the chapter's QR code for a downloadable example.)

STEP 4: Identify the what of the exercise, which should be the desired outcome or topic of focus. Write it atop the matrix so participants can easily refer to it while they unpack the action steps and determine who will be responsible for them. For instance, you might write *What things need to happen for effective makerspace management?* Remember, this activity is most effective when the goal is kept clear.

STEP 5: Identify the action steps and write them in the Do column. For example, here the group might outline specific steps for makerspace management.

STEP 6: For the Who column, identify and list a specific person or type of stakeholder who can address and champion each item in the Do column (Figure 6.6).

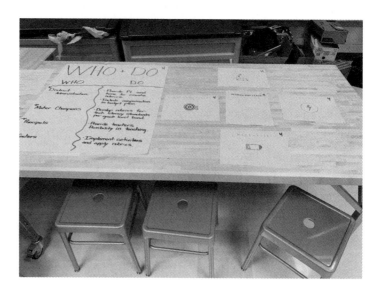

Figure 6.6 Make sure all participants have a clear understanding of the specific goal they are focused on before developing the Who and the Do.

Micro-Credentials: Build Capacity Through Choice

Another way school systems can focus on building educator capacity with maker learning is to create a micro-credentialing process. A powerful method for supporting educators in learning new skills on the job, maker learning micro-credentials offer a personalized, on-demand approach to professional learning. The purpose of a micro-credential format is to provide choice in professional learning, while offering learning in digestible bites. This model allows educators to choose a single skill-based micro-credential or a complete micro-credential pathway to earn recognition for multiple skills. The process of earning micro-credentials is quite efficient for developing and demonstrating new skills on the job.

The Maker Learning Micro-Credential Process

The choice of micro-credential skill they want to earn is up to the individual educator, but each micro-credential class should follow the same simple three-step format:

1. **LEARN.** In the Learn phase of professional learning activities, educators review examples, articles, videos, and links to new information on the skill they are developing.

2. **CREATE.** During the Create phase, educators apply their new learning to create an activity that will be used with students. Templates and examples should be provided.

3. **IMPLEMENT AND SHARE.** Educators can see the impact of their professional learning and work in a timely matter by implementing their creation with students in real time.

Student artifacts should be collected and submitted for review in order to evaluate the quality and outcome of the student learning experience to help determine if the educator effectively applied their newly developed skill. If successful, educators earn a micro-credential and receive a shareable digital badge that can be used to enhance their portfolio or resume, and validate their unique skills (Figure 6.7).

To provide ongoing support and feedback and deepen the professional learning process, be sure to make coaching available throughout all three phases.

If you work in a school system that offers graphic design opportunities for students, there is potential to provide an authentic design challenge to students. Design students can use their skills, tools, and talents to create authentic digital badges. This process involves working with students to understand the vision of the micro-credential program, the audience, and what each micro-credential stands for. It is amazing to see what powerful graphics students can produce!

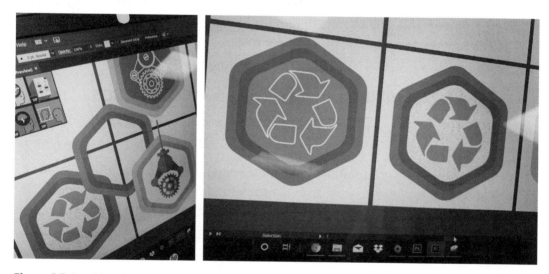

Figure 6.7 Provide educators with digital badges upon successful completion of their micro-credentials.

Table 6.4 illustrates a sample pathway to provide to an educator embarking on a micro-credential process.

TABLE 6.4 Sample Maker Learning Micro-Credential Pathway

PLAN & THINK	SPACE & RESOURCES	BUILD & TEST
Maker learning is based on the ability to identify and investigate problems worth solving while reflecting on one's own process. These skills are the foundation of a successful maker learning experience.	Tools and capacities for maker learning are quite diverse. Knowing how to navigate maker resources with safety and intention is key to success.	Powerful prototypes take on many different forms. Learn the tools and develop the skills to bring your ideas to life.
Micro-credentials for building these skills: • Problem Investigator • Sketching Expert • Reflection Guru	Micro-credentials for building these skills: • Safety Specialist • Repurposing Master	Micro-credentials for building these skills: • Prototyping Ninja • Prototype Tester • 3D Model Master • 3D Printer Wizard • Robotics Rockstar • Code Developer • Website Designer • Video Producer • Photo-Graphic Visionary

Create an Executive Summary Overview

When getting ready to launch your maker micro-credential pathways, explicitly communicate information about your micro-credential program to all educators. Specifically, having a clear executive summary and overview is powerful. The following is a sample executive summary. You can find a downloadable version and more information about micro-credentialing in the Chapter 6 Resources.

SAMPLE: EXECUTIVE SUMMARY OVERVIEW

OBJECTIVE

Provide flexible, personalized, competency-based professional learning opportunities to support educators in gaining understanding, skills, and confidence when developing student experiences in the areas of maker learning and design thinking.

GOALS

- Provide professional learning opportunities in an on-demand, online format.
- Provide a consistent format for helping educators efficiently connect new learning with classroom implementation and student data collection.
- Collect qualitative and quantitative data that reflects teacher skill level and student artifacts as evidence of teachers' newly developed skills.
- Curate examples of powerful maker learning outcomes.
- Engage educators in professional learning that is competency-based.

SOLUTION

The [School System Name] is offering a flexible learning process to support educators in learning new skills on the job. Maker Learning and Design Flexible Professional Development Opportunities are personalized, and educators can choose a single specialty skill or a complete pathway for earning recognition for multiple skills. To demonstrate skills successfully, educators must collect and submit student artifacts for review. Because this process is focused on intentional instructional design and student data, it is a perfect choice for educators wanting to develop a portfolio for licensed educator compensation. If successful, educators will earn recognition and receive a shareable digital badge that can be used to enhance a portfolio or resume, and validate unique skills.

PROJECT OUTLINE

- Identify specific skills necessary for high-impact maker learning and design thinking experiences.
- Align each of these skills to the ISTE and *[state]* Department of Public Instruction Information & Technology Literacy standards *[if available]*.
- Support opportunities for teacher choice in skill development by offering opportunities to develop a single skill or complete a comprehensive maker learning pathway.
- Leverage Google Classroom as an online system to provide flexible access to professional learning.
- Collaborate with professionals who have an expertise in specific maker tools, techniques, and technologies to develop the professional learning curriculum.
- Structure every professional learning opportunity to include the following consistent format:
    - Learn: In the Learn section of the class, educators review examples, articles, videos, and links to new information on the skill they are developing.
    - Create: During the Create section, educators apply their new learning to create an activity that will be used with students. Templates and examples are provided.
    - Implement and Share: Educators can see the impact of their professional learning and work in a timely matter by implementing their creation with students in real time.
        - Collect and analyze evidence of teacher learning and student outcomes.
- Provide a shareable digital badge when individuals have successfully completed a competency-based professional learning experience to create a culture that celebrates and supports maker learning as an instructional practice.

Maker Roadmap: Guide the Journey

Continuous improvement is a journey. To help educators evaluate and refine the learner experience, it is important to provide a map for this work, such as the Maker Roadmap in Figure 6.8. Identifying where, when, and how design process and computational thinking fits within current curriculum can be complex and, for some people, downright intimidating. Whether you are just starting out on the journey of maker learning or advancing your existing inclusive maker culture, providing educators a bird's-eye view of the complete maker experience is pivotal to help guide and pace their work. The Maker Roadmap supports educators as they make decisions and monitor their progress.

In addition, as noted in Chapter 4, teachers can use the Maker Roadmap to offer learners a pathway to develop their executive functioning skills, plan, and assess the progress of their own work. Learners can use the Maker Roadmap to identify where they are in the design process, who they are on this journey with, key places they will want to visit along the way, and strategies to help them stay on pace and overcome any roadblocks and challenges. Encourage students to revisit their roadmap consistently. A few more tips to consider are:

- Review the Maker Roadmap at each phase of the design process to encourage students to make sure they are on track and know where they are going next.

- Remind students to review the Maker Roadmap when they are lost or stuck. This map also provides guidance for determining pacing and making adjustments when implementation feels stagnant.

- Encourage students to review the Maker Roadmap when they are setting goals for their design work.

MAKER ROADMAP: THE MAKER JOURNEY
The design process is a journey. As you navigate this journey, use the Maker Roadmap to help guide and pace yourself. This roadmap can be used to help you identify where you are in your design process, who you are on this journey with, key places you will want to stop at along the way, and strategies to help you stay on pace and overcome any roadblocks and challenges you may face.

Tips for Using the Roadmap	
<ul><li>Review the Maker Roadmap at each phase of the design process to make sure you are on track and know where you are going.</li><li>Review this map when you are lost or stuck.</li><li>Review this map to help set goals for your design work or create a timeline of important deadlines.</li></ul>	
Current Location: Where Am I Now?	**Questions to Ask Myself:**<ul><li>What do I need to know and do? What are my learning intentions?<ul><li>I can…</li></ul></li><li>What is the design challenge?</li><li>At what stage of the design process am I?<ul><li>Form an empathetic connection: What, why, and who am I making for?</li><li>Research, observations, interviews</li><li>Problem statement</li><li>Possible solutions</li><li>Sketch my prototype solution</li><li>Make my prototype solution</li><li>Test my prototype solution</li><li>Iterate and make improvements</li><li>Launch my final prototype solution</li></ul></li></ul>
Travel Companions	**Who Is with Me on This Journey?**<ul><li>My peers</li><li>My design team</li><li>Partnerships (if applicable)</li><li>Teachers</li><li>Family</li></ul>
Places to Go!	**What Stage of the Design Process Is Next?**<ul><li>Form an empathetic connection: What, why, and who am I making for?</li><li>Research, observations, interviews</li><li>Problem statement</li><li>Possible solutions</li><li>Sketch my prototype solution</li><li>Make my prototype solution</li><li>Test my prototype solution, get feedback</li><li>Iterate and make improvements</li><li>Launch my final prototype solution</li></ul>

continues

MAKER ROADMAP: THE MAKER JOURNEY	

Speed Limits	**What Can I Do to Make Sure I'm Going the Right Speed?**
	• Identify deadlines on my class calendar
	• Review project checklists
	• Set personal goals and timelines for my work
	• Create a schedule to help me accomplish my goals
	• Plan for how much time I am supposed to spend at a specific stage or how long a task should take me
	  • Do I have bigger items (projects/tests) that will demand more of my time?
	  • Do I have events in my personal life or tasks that I need to account for in my planning to make sure I can complete my work?

Pit Stops	**What Resources Can Help Me Navigate My Journey?** **What Places Should I Stop At or Visit Along the Way?** • Visit my class calendar or project deadlines list • Check in at online spaces that support my work (learning management system or workflow tool) • Visit the makerspace • Ask or message my teacher for help • Take time to think, reflect, and reboot if needed • Gather feedback from peers or partners along the way
Roadblocks	**What Do I Do When I'm Facing a Challenge in My Work?** • Check the online learning spaces for extra resources • Meet with my teacher • Find additional or supplementary resources to help me • Ask a peer or design teammate to think about any challenges with me and brainstorm solutions
Roadside Assistance	**When I Run Into a Challenge, Who Can Help and What Can I Do?** • Ask my teacher for help • Look at any supplementary resources on my class site or online learning space • Look back at past work that I have completed • Check in with a peer • Use sentence stems to help think about what I want to ask for or need help with

Figure 6.8 The Maker Roadmap is a powerful tool for educators as well as students. This roadmap provides users with an opportunity to monitor their work progress, set goals for pacing, and visualize key action steps during the design process.

Next Steps and Reflection

This playbook has presented activities, strategies, and resources that you can use (or encourage others to use) to develop your own inclusive maker learning culture. Whether you work at the classroom, building, or district level, there are a variety of strategies shared in this book to engage stakeholders in active participation and cognitive engagement. No matter if the learners you work with are young people or adults, it is important that you consider how to address learner variability at different stages of the process for creating and supporting an inclusive maker learning environment. You'll find plenty of resources to help you by scanning each chapter's QR code.

Chapter 6 Resources

In closing, I invite you to reflect on the list of questions on the signs and signals for success you first encountered in the Introduction. Revisit these through your journey of supporting an inclusive maker learning culture to stay focused on your goals.

 CREATING AN INCLUSIVE VISION

Ask yourself...

- How will you provide opportunities for stakeholders to visualize inclusive maker learning?
- How will you use your definition of maker learning to help stakeholders articulate connections between student learning goals and engaging learners in a deliberate design process?
- What are the essential qualities and characteristics learners should experience during maker and design work?

 BUILDING EDUCATOR SKILLS

Be sure to consider...

- What skills do stakeholders need to possess in order to be accountable for creating inclusive maker environments?
- How will you encourage stakeholders to regulate their own learning when building new skills?

IDENTIFYING INCENTIVES

Evaluate opportunities by asking...

- How will you create entry points into inclusive maker learning experiences that engage the interests of all stakeholders?
- How can your process provide options for stakeholders to act strategically?

PROCURING RESOURCES

Be sure to examine the following...

- How will you identify resources (physical, time, social, or human) that sustain effort and motivation while building an inclusive maker learning culture?
- How will you introduce resources in ways that help stakeholders perceive the opportunities these resources bring to all learners?
- In an ideal world, how would you like stakeholders to physically respond in the makerspace or with maker resources?

PARTICIPATING IN ONGOING ACTION PLANNING

Unpack the following...

- What specific action steps can specific stakeholders deliver?
- How will you organize the timeline of your work to ensure that all stakeholders receive appropriate learning, training, and practice?
- How will you engage in ongoing progress monitoring and provide mastery-oriented feedback to stakeholders at various points in your process?

References

Andrews, M. (2018, November 25). Accessibility = innovation. *Prototypr.* **blog.prototypr.io/accessibility-innovation-20912107fc4e**

Aoun, J. E. (2017). *Robot-proof: Higher education in the age of artificial intelligence.* The MIT Press.

Brand, W. (2017). *Visual thinking: Empowering people & organizations through visual collaboration.* BIS Publishers.

Brand, W. (2019). *Visual doing: Applying visual thinking in your day-to-day business.* BIS Publishers.

Brown, T. (2009). *Change by design: How design thinking transforms organizations and inspires innovation.* Collins Business.

Carleton, L., & Marzano, R. J. (2010). *Vocabulary games for the classroom.* Marzano Research Laboratory.

CAST. (2018). *Universal Design for Learning Guidelines, version 2.2.* **udlguidelines.cast.org**

Daugherty, P. R., & Wilson, H. J. (2018). *Human + machine: Reimagining work in the age of AI.* Harvard Business Review Press.

Doorley, S., & Witthoft, S. (2012). *Make space: How to set the stage for creative collaboration.* John Wiley & Sons.

Fisher, D., & Frey, N. (2014). *Better learning through structured teaching: A framework for the gradual release of responsibility, 2nd edition.* ASCD.

Fisher, D., Frey, N., Bustamante, V., & Hattie, J. (2021). *The assessment playbook for distance and blended learning: Measuring student learning in any setting.* Corwin.

Fitzpatrick, R. (2013). *The mom test: How to talk to customers & learn if your business is a good idea when everyone is lying to you.* CreateSpace Independent Publishing Platform.

Fleming, L. (2018). *The kickstart guide to making great makerspaces.* Corwin.

Grant, K., & Pérez, L. (2018). *Dive into UDL: Immersive practices to develop expert learners.* ISTE.

Graves, C., & Graves, A. (2017). *The big book of makerspace projects: Inspiring makers to experiment, create, and learn.* McGraw-Hill Education.

Gray, D., Brown, S., & Macanufo, J. (2010). *Gamestorming: A playbook for innovators, rulebreakers, and changemakers.* O'Reilly Media.

Guskey, T. R. (2000). *Evaluating professional development.* Corwin Press.

Himmele, P., & Himmele, W. (2017). *Total participation techniques: Making every student an active learner, 2nd edition*. ASCD.

Hohmann, L. (2007). *Innovation games: Creating breakthrough products through collaborative play*. Addison-Wesley.

International Society for Technology in Education [ISTE]. (2016). ISTE Standards for Students. **iste.org/standards/for-students**

Knoster, T., Villa, R., & Thousand, J. (2000). *A framework for thinking about systems change*. In R. Villa & J. Thousands (Eds.) *Restructuring for caring and effective education: Piecing the puzzle together, 2nd edition* (pp. 93–128). Paul H. Brookes Publishing Co.

Microsoft. (2018). Inclusive design. **microsoft.com/design/inclusive**

Nair, P. (2014). *Blueprint for tomorrow: Redesigning schools for student-centered learning*. Harvard Education Press.

Rubino, S. C., Hazenberg, W., & Huisman, M. (2012). *75 tools for creative thinking* [Card deck]. BIS Publishers.

Sinek, S. (2017). *Find your why: A practical guide for discovering purpose for you and your team*. Portfolio/Penguin.

Stobaugh, R. (2019). *Fifty strategies to boost cognitive engagement: Creating a thinking culture in the classroom*. Solution Tree Press.

Teagle Foundation. (n.d.). *Ingredients for sustainable change* [Infographic]. **teaglefoundation.org/Teagle/media/GlobalMediaLibrary/documents/resources/IngredientsForSustainableChange.pdf?ext=.pdf**

Thornburg, D. D. (2007). *Campfires in cyberspace: Primordial metaphors for learning in the 21st century*. Thornburg Center for Professional Development. **digitalsandbox.weebly.com/uploads/5/5/8/8/5588196/campfires.pdf**

Wiggins, G., & McTighe, J. (2005). *Understanding by design, expanded second edition*. ASCD.

Wiggins, G., & McTighe, J. (2012). *The understanding by design guide to advanced concepts in creating and reviewing units*. ASCD.

Index

A

action and expression, resources for, 97-101
action planning, xv, 188-191, 199-200, 204-206, 216
Adobe Spark collaborative creation tool, 46, 167, 178
Agency, Authenticity, Audience (3 As), 12
analysis, guiding, 130-131
Andrews, Mischa, xi
annotation tools, 180
Aoun, Joseph E., 2-3
attention, grabbing, 126-127
audience, engaging with, 166-167
audiences and users, targeting, 116-127
audio recording tools, using, 124
automation, Computational Thinker Standard, 8

B

barriers to inclusive learning, identifying, 42-44
Blueprint for Tomorrow: Redesigning Schools for Student-Centered Learning, 83
brainstorming activities, 5, 11, 29-30, 43-46, 49, 141, 204-206
breakthroughs, creating, 42
Brown, Tim, 17

C

cameras, using, 124
"Campfires in Cyberspace," 83
Canva graphic design tool, 46, 167
Canvas learning management system, 68
capacity, building through choice, 207-211
Card Sort Tool, 173
CAST (Center for Applied Special Technology), x

challenges, customizing, 14. *See also* maker challenge
change, supporting, 171, 187-191
Change by Design, 17
Check for Understanding Cards, 91-92
checklists and rubrics, 73
choice, using to build capacity, 207-211
clarity of expectations, techniques for, 73
A Class Divided, 127
Clips, 113, 152, 180
collaboration. *See also* interaction with peers
and feedback, 84-85
scaffold opportunities for, 74-76
collaborative creation tools, 46
collaborative documents, using, 54, 139
Collaborative Group Card, 93
collaborative whiteboard, using, 44
Comic Life, 178, 180
Computational Thinker, ISTE Standard for Students, 7-10
confidence, increasing, 150-151
connectedness, showing, 112
connecting dots and building capacity, 39-41
connection, scaffold opportunities for, 74-76. *See also* empathetic connections
cover story, creating headline for, 47
credibility, assessing, 132-134
crosswalk tables, downloading, xiii
culture of inclusive maker learning. *See also* maker culture
 brain writing, 28-30
 brainstorming, 34-36
 dot voting, 34-36
 repeat and refine, 30-32
 target storming, 28-30
 tell me why, 32-34

D

Da Vinci, 167
data
 evaluating, 127-134
 and evaluating professional learning, 194-195
 for informing action planning, 199-200
 and making decisions, 194-195
data analysis, strategy for, 129-130
data collection, Computational Thinker Standard, 7
data literacy, 3
de Bobo, Edward, 161
decisions, making, 194-200
define term, explained, 105
design and building, considerations, xi-xii
design portfolio sample, 77
design process
 components of, 12
 Innovative Designer Standard, 5
 learning artifacts for, 70-72
 strategies for, 104-106
design skills, considering, 187
design studios and makerspaces, xii
design terms, teaching, 106-108
design thinking process, 60-62, 105
designer's reasoning, evaluating, 146-148
digital learning and 1:1 programming, 40
digital storyboards, creating, 178, 180
digital tools, Innovative Designer Standard, 5
discrimination lesson, example of, 127
distraction of students, avoiding, 85
diverse perspectives, embracing, 39
documenting maker learning process, 70, 76-77
Dossetto, Fio, 122
dot voting, 34-36, 57, 121, 140

E

educator skills, building, xiv, 215
edpuzzle, 120
effect size, measuring for strategies and methods, 198-199
Elliot, Jane, 127
empathetic connections, 119, 124-126. *See also* connection
empathize term, defined, 105
end game, determining, 186
engagement, resources for, 79-89
evaluate term, explained, 105
evaluation strategies, 161-167
evaluation term, explained, 106
Everyone Can Code—Apple WWDC 2016, 20
executive summary overview, creating, 209-211
experiences
    gaining insight into, 177-179
    learning through storytelling, 175-177
expert learners, x, 75-76
Explain Everything screencasting tool, 112-113, 128
expression and action, resources for, 97-101

F

face-to-face process, mirroring, 29
feedback and collaboration, 84-85
feedback process, reflecting on, 164-165
Find Your Why, 170-171
Flipgrid videos, 61, 107, 156, 159

G

GarageBand, 124, 130
Go Remote sidebars
    Tools & Techniques to Support Collaboration Everywhere, xiv
    and virtual settings, xiii
goal-setting sample, 72
Google Classroom, 68-69
Google Docs, 35, 49, 56, 117, 127, 139, 146, 173
Google Draw, 44, 113, 140, 173, 205
Google Forms, 35, 56, 59, 124, 137, 140, 146, 148, 156, 159, 182
Google Jamboard app, 10, 44, 107, 112, 121, 126-127, 130-131, 135, 140, 150, 156, 159, 165, 173, 205
Google Meet, 139, 167
Google Sheets, 165
Google Sites, 46, 148, 152, 167
Google Slides, 29, 31, 61, 107, 126-127, 131, 139-140, 152, 173, 202
graphic organizers, providing for students, 112, 138, 147, 160, 205
graphics, creating virtually, 44
GRASPS (Goal, Role, Audience, Situation, Purpose, Standards) maker design challenge, 15-16
Gray, Brown, & Macanufo, 143
group card, 93
groups, working in, 161

H

headline, creating for cover story, 47
high-impact makerspaces, 66-67
Himmele & Himmele, 178
How to Make a Cardboard Prototype, 20

I

"I Can" statements, 73
ideal components, envisioning, 44-47
ideas
    comparing, 109-111
    generating and evaluating, 139-141
    moving around digitally, 112
ideation, 105, 117
IDEO U resources, 105
images and stories, sharing, 113
iMovie Trailers, 113, 167, 180
incentives, identifying, xv, 216
Inclusive: A Microsoft Design Toolkit, xi
inclusive maker learning
    defining, 10-11, 171
    developing understanding of, 28-36, 177-179
    documenting process of, 76-77
    environment and UDL, 78
    envisioning future state of components for, 44-47
    evaluating, 179-181
    identifying barriers to, 42-44
    incentives for engaging in, 187
    launch assessment, 191-193
    resources, 188
    unpacking, 171
    videos, 19-21
    vision for, 187
inclusive spaces, creating, 66-67
inclusive vision, creating, 215
inductive reasoning strategy, 115-116
infographics, creating, 167
informational sources, distinguishing, 132-134
initiatives, connecting, 39-41
inquiry, sparking, 126-127
interaction with peers, 131-134. *See also* collaboration; peer feedback
interview data analysis skills, 123
interviews, unpacking responses from, 130-131
investing time, 170
iPad's Screen Recording feature, 128
Is It Making activity, 11-14
ISTE Innovative Designer Playlist, 21
ISTE Standards for Educators
    Analyst, 32, 36, 46, 55, 59, 177, 179
    Citizen, 179
    Collaborator, 29, 31, 46, 50, 53, 57, 173, 175, 181, 201, 204
    Designer, 48, 177
    Facilitator, 29, 48, 55
    Leader, 31, 43, 175, 204
    Learner, 43, 173, 201
ISTE Standards for Students. *See also* students
    Computational Thinker, 7-10, 111, 115, 146, 149
    Creative Communicator, 116, 128-129, 131, 145-146, 149-150, 166
    Digital Citizen, 133, 150
    Empowered Learner, 135-136, 138-139, 150
    Global Collaborator, 138-139, 141, 143, 161, 164

INDEX

Innovative Designer, 4–6, 106, 116, 123, 125–126, 141, 143, 145, 152, 155–157
Knowledge Constructor, 108–109, 111, 113–115, 119, 121, 123, 125–126, 128–131, 133, 135

K

Keynote collaborative creation tool, using, 46, 61, 107, 127, 140, 152, 202
Knoster, Villa, & Thousand, 187
Knoster Model for Managing Complex Change, 187–188, 200. *See also* surveys

L

leaders, types of, 170
learners, types of, 40
learning intentions. *See also* professional learning
  communicating, 72–74
  making visible, 94–95
learning spaces, maximizing use of, 83
LMS (learning management system), 68–69

M

maker challenge, increasing clarity of, 15–16. *See also* challenges
Maker Champions, 22–26, 182
maker culture. *See also* culture of inclusive maker learning
  defining, 4
  ISTE Standards for Students, 4–10
  literacies for success, 2–4
Maker Manifesto, 26–27
Maker Roadmap, 212–214
maker tools and capacities, 12
makerspace content, guide to, 88
makerspaces. *See also* virtual workspaces
  categorizing materials in, 94
  cleaning up, 85
  content, 88
  and design studios, xii
  high-impact, 66–67
  use guidelines for, 101

making
  defining, 11–12
  focusing on the why, 14–15
  sample prompts, 12–14
materials, categorizing in spaces, 94
McTighe, Jay, 15
metacognitive tasks, 73
metaphors, creating, 108–109
methods, measuring effect size of, 198–199
micro-credential skill, 207–209
Microsoft Design Toolkit, 22
Microsoft PowerPoint, 61, 107, 152, 202
MindMup, 112
movement and auditory breaks, 87

N

Nair, Prakash, 83
Nearpod app, 59
needs, basing resources on, 57–60
next-step goal setting sample, 72
Not Everything Makes the Cut, 21
Notes app, using, 31, 46
Notes (for iPad or iPhone), 113, 142, 205
Numbers, using, 29, 124, 165

O

observation skills, developing, 123–126
observations, unpacking responses from, 130–131
organizing learning systems, 68–69. *See also* Quote It, Code It! graphic organizer

P

Padlet, 29, 46, 112, 121, 130–131, 135, 137, 142, 148, 156, 159, 165, 173, 202
  Reply and Rate features, 34
  Shelf format, 56
Pages app, 29, 46, 124, 127, 140, 178, 180
Paper, 142
patterns of thinking, developing, 50–53
PDFs, annotating, 46
Pear Deck app, 59

peer feedback, scaffolding, 157. *See also* interaction with peers
perseverance, tolerance for, 6
perspectives of events, exploring, 130–131
photos
  annotations, 159
  taking, 152
Planning a Disaster strategy, 48–49. *See also* problems
PollUnit online tool, 44
portfolios for students, 98
Post-it App, 137
PowerSchool Learning, 68
prioritizing
  actions, 204–206
  resources, 55–57
problem definitions, Computational Thinker Standard, 7
problems
  breaking into parts, 8
  defining, 134–143
  exploring, 53–55
process and tools, 40
professional learning. *See also* learning intentions
  diversifying elements of evaluation, 197
  evaluating, 194–200
  programmatic growth, evaluating, 200–206
prototypes, Innovative Designer Standard, 6
prototyping, 16–21, 105–106
provocation, solution to, 105
puzzle pieces, managing, 39–42

Q

QR codes
  Apple Round Pizza Box Ad, 21
  Chapter 1 Resources, 36
  Everyone Can Code—Apple WWDC 2016, 20
  How to Make a Cardboard Prototype, 20
  Introduction Resources, xvi
  ISTE Innovative Designer Playlist, 21
  Meet Molly, the Kid Who Never Stops Inventing GE Commercial, 19

INDEX

QR codes (continued)
  Not Everything Makes the Cut, 21
  Rapid Prototyping: Sketching/Google for Startups, 20
  UDL Guidelines, x
questions, crafting, 121–122
Quote It, Code It! graphic organizer, 123. *See also* organizing learning systems

R

Rapid Prototyping: Sketching/Google for Startups, 20
reflection and self-assessment sample, 71
representation, resources for, 90–96
research, conducting, 127–134
resource prioritization strategy, 55–57
resources
  Accountable Talk Cards, 84–85
  for action and expression, 97–101
  Action-Inspiring Signage, 86
  Appropriate Use Guidelines for Makerspaces, 101
  basing on needs, 57–60
  Categorize Materials in the Space, 94
  Choice Auditory and Movement Breaks, 87
  Clean-up Job Cards, 85
  Design Thinking Process Signage, 96
  for engagement, 79–89
  Gathering Student Check for Understanding Card Responses, 91–92
  Getting to Know the Makerspace Walkabout Activity, 89
  At-a-Glance Guide to Makerspace Content, 88
  Grab-and-Go Check for Understanding Cards, 91
  for maker learning, 188
  Making Learning Intentions Visible, 94–95
  procuring, xv, 216
  for representation, 90–96
  Self-Regulation Charts, 79–80
  Shared Work Agreements, 81–82
  Space Configurations Guide, 82–83
  Student Collaborative Group Card, 93
  Student Portfolios, 98
  Student Work Showcase, 100
  Target Storming Activity, 99
results, identifying, 195–196
Ripple Effect, incorporating, 178
Robot-Proof: Higher Education in the Age of Artificial Intelligence, 2
routines, fostering for students. *See* student routines, 68–72
rubrics and checklists, 73

S

scaffold opportunities
  Claims, Evidence, Reasons strategy, 128–129
  connection and collaboration, 74–76
  peer feedback, 157
  Sketching Checklist strategy, 144
Schoology learning management system, 68
screencasting tools, 128, 152
screenshot capabilities, 142, 152
Seesaw workflow tool, 68–69, 107
self-assessment and reflection sample, 71
self-reflection tasks, 73
sharing images and stories, 113
showcasing student work, 100
ShowMe screencasting tool, 113, 128
signage
  action-inspiring, 86
  design thinking process, 96
Sinek, Simon, 170–171
sketching apps, 205
skill building, supporting, 3, 9–10
slide decks, 126
Smore, 167
solutions
  ideating, 134–143
  providing for provocations, 105
SoundTrap, 124, 130
sources, reliability of, 130–131
stakeholder groups, building understanding across, 170–171
sticky notes, 121, 137
stories and images, sharing, 113
storytelling, learning about experiences from, 175–177
strategies
  Accountable Talk Stems for Analysis, 150–151
  Affinity Diagram: Cluster and Rate Solutions, 136–137
  Assessing Credibility Jigsaw, 132–134
  Assumption Busting, 181–183
  Both Sides of the Story, 50–53
  Brain Writing and Target Storming, 28–30
  Brainstorming and Dot Voting, 34–36
  Campfire, 175–177
  Card Sort—Inductive Reasoning, 115–116
  Claims, Evidence, Reasons, 128–129
  Comparing Ideas, 109–111
  Consensogram, 139–141
  Crafting Questions, 121–122
  Creating an Inclusive Vision, xiv
  Creating Ideas, 109–111
  Creating Metaphors, 108–109
  to cultivate expert learners, 75–76
  A Day in the Life of a Maker, 177–179
  design challenge, 106–116
  Empathy Canvas, 201–204
  Evaluating the Designer's Reasoning, 146–148
  Filling in the Gaps, 179–181
  Finding Fiction, 114
  Hear, Think, Wonder, 129–130
  Hear It, See It, Quote It, Code It! 122–124
  Maker Learning and UDL Card Sort, 172–174
  Makerspace Resource Prioritization, 55–57
  Makerspace Walkabout, 155–156
  Making for Who, 116–118
  measuring effect size of, 198–199

INDEX

Methods for Sharing Student Work with an Authentic Audience, 166-167
Mom Test, 119-120
navigating, xiii-xiv
On the Cover, 44-47
Overheard Quotes, 130-131
phases of design process, 104-106
Planning a Disaster, 48-49
Prototyping Accountable Talk Stems, 156-157
Prototyping Process Checklist, 151-154
Puzzle Stories, 113
Questioning and Peer Review, 149-150
Questions and Comparisons, 131-132
Repeat and Refine, 30-32
SCAMPER, 157-160
Scavenger Hunt, 60-62
Six Thinking Hats: Launching Your Work, 161-163
Sketching Checklist, 144-146
Solution Storming, 141-142
State and Rank Possible Solutions, 138-139
SWOT Analysis, 143
Taken by Surprise, 126-127
Teaching Key Design Terms, 106-108
Tell Me Why, 32-34
Thinking Cube, 164-165
True for Who, 57-60
Unpacking the Boxes, 42-43
Visual Thinking, 124-126
The What, The Who, The Do, 204-206
Where To? 53-55
Which One Doesn't Belong, 111-112
Writing Problem Statements, 134-135
student innovation, redefining opportunities for, 2-10
student routines, fostering, 68-72
student work, sharing, 100, 166-167
students. *See also* ISTE Standards for Students
considering skills for, 3
interaction with peers, 131-134
success criteria, identifying, 2-4, 193-196
surveys, assessing maker learning launch, 191-193. *See also* Knoster Model for Managing Complex Change

T

talk cards, 84-85
target user or audience, identifying, 116-127
T-charts, using, 33-34, 176
teacher actions and initiatives, 41
teacher checklist, high-impact virtual maker learning tasks, 74
teacher planning, 40
technological literacy, 3
templates, using, 49, 129-130, 134, 203
thinking
  chunking, 112
  making visible, 91
thinking aloud, capturing, 128
thinking patterns, developing, 50-53, 150-151
Thornburg, David, 83
time, investing, 170
types of learners, 40

U

UDL (Universal Design for Learning)
  and access, x-xi
  Action & Expression guidelines, 16
  creation of, x
  in maker learning environment, 78
UDL Guidelines
  Access layer, x
  implementation of, 77
UDL principles, examples of, 172-174
understanding, building across stakeholders, 170-171
The Understanding by Design Guide to Advanced Concepts in Creating and Reviewing Units, 15
use guidelines for makerspaces, 101
users and audiences, targeting, 116-127

V

verbal ideation, 117
video reflections, constructing, 152
videoconferencing tools, 34, 51, 54, 117, 132, 134-135, 137, 139, 162, 177-178
videos
  creating, 167, 180
  template for, 129-130
  using Flipgrid for, 61
  for visualizing maker learning, 19-21
virtual gallery walks, 46
virtual makerspace, steps to, 67
virtual workspaces, high-impact, 67-77. *See also* makerspaces
vision, making inclusive, xiv
visuals, creating, 152
voice recording tools, 117
voice-to-text features, 117

W

Wallet Project, 117
Webex, 139
website creation tools, 167
Weebly, 167
WeVideo, 152, 167
wheelofnames.com, 120
whiteboard tools, 34, 44, 137, 140, 150, 177
why, focusing on, 14-15, 170-171
Wiggins, Grant, 15
work agreements, sharing, 81-82
workflow tools, 68-69
worst-case scenarios, averting, 49

Y

YouTube, 167

Z

Zoom, 54, 139, 167

IF YOU LIKED THIS BOOK, CHECK OUT THESE GREAT ISTE TITLES!

All books available in print and ebook formats at iste.org/books

Dive Into UDL: Immersive Practices to Develop Expert Learners
BY KENDRA GRANT AND LUIS PEREZ

Learn how to incorporate accessible learning materials and technologies into your instructional design to ensure choice for learners and help them develop into independent, motivated expert learners.

iste.org/DiveIntoUDL

The New Assistive Tech: Make Learning Awesome for All!
BY CHRISTOPHER R. BUGAJ

This playful yet professional book is designed to help educators select, acquire and implement technology to help all students, but especially those with special needs.

iste.org/NewAssistiveTech

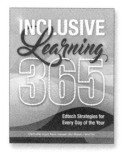

Inclusive Learning 365: Edtech Strategies for Every Day of the Year
BY CHRISTOPHER R. BUGAJ, KAREN JANOWSKI, MIKE MAROTTA AND BETH POSS

Designed to be read one day — and page — at a time, this book from four inclusive learning experts offers 365 strategies for implementing technology to design inclusive experiences.

iste.org/Inclusive365

Building a K-12 STEM Lab: A Step-by-Step Guide for School Leaders and Tech Coaches
BY DEBORAH KANTOR NAGLER AND MARTHA OSEI-YAW

Get insights and clear guidelines for developing the robust partnerships and processes you need to build a successful STEM lab in your school.

iste.org/STEMLab

LEARN AS A TEAM WITH ISTE BOOKS!
ISTE's bulk books program makes team-based PD a breeze, and you'll save 35% or more off the retail price when you order large quantities. Email books@iste.org for details.

ISTE members get 25% off every day!